Northern Edge in association
with Neil McPherson for the Finborough Theatre presents

The World Premiere

# 17

by **Dameon Garnett**

# FINBOROUGH | THEATRE

First performed at the Finborough Theatre as a staged reading as part of *Vibrant 2013 – A Festival of Finborough Playwrights*: Saturday, 19 October 2013.

First performance at the Finborough Theatre: Sunday, 20 July 2014.

# 17

by **Dameon Garnett**

*Cast in order of speaking*

| | |
|---|---|
| Lisa | **Catherine Harvey** |
| Daniel | **Paul Regan** |
| Scott | **Ryan Blackburn** |
| Leo | **Greg Fossard** |

The action takes place in Liverpool, present day.

The performance lasts approximately eighty minutes.

There will be no interval.

| | |
|---|---|
| Director | **Emma Faulkner** |
| Designer | **Bethany Wells** |
| Lighting Designer | **Peter Harrison** |
| Sound Designer | **Max Pappenheim** |
| Associate Designer | **Lauren Tata** |
| Producer | **Max Milner** |
| Producer | **Winona Navin-Holder** |

Our patrons are respectfully reminded that, in this intimate theatre, any noise such as rustling programmes, talking or the ringing of mobile phones may distract the actors and your fellow audience-members.

We regret there is no admittance or re-admittance to the auditorium whilst the performance is in progress.

*17* is performed in repertoire and on the set of *This Was A Man*, designed by Simon Kenny, which plays Tuesday to Saturday evenings, and Saturday and Sunday matinees, until Saturday, 2 August 2014.

**Ryan Blackburn** | Scott

Trained at East 15 Acting School.

Theatre includes *The Boyband* and *Fitness Freaks* (Writer's Avenue at Pleasance London), *Living The Dream* (Writer's Avenue at Soho Theatre), *Pale In The Shade* (Tamasha at the Bush Theatre), *Inspector Clueless and The Missing Materials* (National Tour for Quantum Theatre) and *Lifestars* (Everyman Theatre, Liverpool).

Television includes *Britain's Secret Homes*.

**Greg Fossard** | Leo

Trained at the Royal Central School of Speech and Drama.

Theatre includes *Dreamboats and Petticoats* (National Tour), *Avenue Q* (Korea), *Little Voice* (National Tour), *Dick Whittington* (Courtyard Theatre, Hereford), *Our House* – 10th anniversary gala concert (Savoy Theatre), *Numberjacks* (National Tour), *Spring Awakening* (English Theatre Frankfurt), *Twopence to Cross the Mersey* (Empire Theatre, Liverpool) and *Les Miserables* (National Tour).

Film includes *My Beautiful Son*.

Television includes *Nice Guy Eddie*.

Recordings and Radio include *Spring Awakening* (English Theatre, Frankfurt, cast recording) and *Till the Words Come Back*.

**Catherine Harvey** | Lisa

Productions at the Finborough Theatre include *Quality Street*, *Unburied* as part of *Vibrant 2010 – An Anniversary Festival of Finborough Playwrights*, and as a member of the Finborough Theatre's Literary Development Ensemble.

Trained at the Royal Central School of Speech and Drama.

Theatre includes *Geisha Girls – Bush Beano*, *The Purification Ritual of the Sacred Nymphs of Natterjack – Bush Bazaar* (Bush Theatre), *New Views* (National Theatre), *The Ring of Truth, Alison's House* (Orange Tree Theatre, Richmond), *The Comedy Project* (Soho Theatre), *Humble Boy*, *Nightfall* (both tours of the UK and Ireland for London Classic Theatre), *My Balloon Beats Your Astronaut* (Papatango), *Les Enfants du Paradis* (Arcola Theatre), *An Ideal Husband* (Clwyd Theatr Cymru), *Pericles* (Ludlow Festival), the title role in *Deirdre of the Sorrows* (Riverside Studios), *Charley's Aunt* (Norwich Playhouse) and *Erasmus Montanus* (Greenwich Studio Theatre – *Time Out* Critics' Choice Season at BAC).

Television includes *Restless, Emmerdale*, *Where the Heart Is*, *Casualty*, *Judge John Deed*, *Red Dwarf* and the BAFTA-nominated series *A Wing and a Prayer*. Film includes *Oscar and Lucinda*.

Radio includes *Poetry Please, With Great Pleasure, Words and Music, Night Waves, The Verb, Orchestra Paloma, Hans Christian Andersen, 43 Years in the Third Form, Artists With Designs, Doctor Who* and the comedy series *Bangers and Mash*.

Catherine also works as a playwright and a director of stand up comedy.

She won the Redfest new play award for *Angeldust*, which was subsequently longlisted for the Adrienne Benham Award. Her first full-length stage play *Infinite Riches* was produced by the Old Red Lion Theatre, Islington. It was longlisted for Little Brother's Big Opportunity and is published by Playdead Press. Other work includes *Fields Unsown* (co-written with Louise Monaghan for Attic Theatre Company), *The Rialto Burns* (longlisted for the Bruntwood Prize), and short plays at Theatre503, Soho Theatre, Bush Theatre, 24:7 Theatre Festival, Manchester, The Miniaturists at the Arcola Theatre, and three *Doctor Who* audio dramas for Big Finish.

**Paul Regan** | Daniel
Productions at the Finborough Theatre include *Pvt Wars* and Dameon Garnett's *Follow.*
Trained at the Royal Central School of Speech and Drama. Theatre includes *Ma Rainey's Black Bottom*, *The Astonished Heart* and *Still Life* (Liverpool Playhouse), *The Winter's Tale* (Wirral Shakespeare Festival), *Chavasse – VC and Bar* (Liverpool Cathedral), *Waste* (Unity Theatre), *Enter the Clown* (Theatre in the Mill, Bradford), *The Cell* (24:7 Theatre Festival), *Macbeth* (Valley Theatre), *Lonely Meets Lonely* (Didsbury Arts Festival) and *The Ragged Trousered Philanthropists* (Everyman Theatre, Liverpool, and the Chichester Festival Theatre).
Film includes *Day in the Life* and *Esther Kahn*.
Television includes *New Street Law* and *Two Pints of Lager and a Packet of Crisps*.
Radio includes the plays *A Northern Elegy*, *A Painter's Sky Lost in Liverpool* and *Silver Grey* and *Unprotected*.

**Dameon Garnett** | Playwright

Dameon Garnett has had two plays receive their world premieres at the Finborough Theatre – the Time Out Critics' Choice *Break Away* (2005) which starred Tina Malone of *Shameless*, and *Follow* (2008). His first play, *New Year's Day*, was performed at the Royal Court Young Writers' Festival, starring Michael Angelis. He also received a playwriting bursary from the Soho Theatre. In 2013 he was invited to become a member of the Studio Group at the Royal Court Theatre, where he started work on a new play.

**Emma Faulkner** | Director

Productions at the Finborough Theatre include two classics from Northern Ireland – St John Ervine's *John Ferguson* and Sam Thompson's *Over the Bridge*; and the original staged reading of *17* as part of *Vibrant – A Festival of Finborough Playwrights*.
She received the 2010 Regional Theatre Young Director Scheme bursary in association with The Young Vic. Directing includes *London 2012: Glasgow* (Theatre Uncut at the Bussey Building), *Christmas The Musical* (Battersea Mess and Music Hall), *The Sacred Ritual of the Nymphs of Natterjack*, part of Bush Bazaar (Bush Theatre), *Different is Dangerous* (Tamasha), *After the End* (Dundee Rep and Pleasance Edinburgh), *The Miracle* (Dundee Rep), *Forfeit, What Love Is* (Òran Mór and Dundee Rep), *The Ruffian on the Stair, Making Good, Absolute Return* (Orange Tree Theatre, Richmond) and *Knives in Hens* (St Mary's at BAC). Associate Direction includes *Sunshine on Leith* (National Tour). Assistant Direction includes assisting Alan Ayckbourn on *Taking Steps* – as well as *Sleeping Beauty* and *A Doll's House* (Dundee Rep), and *Alison's House, Spring Shakespeare, The Lady or the Tiger* and *The Ring of Truth* (Orange Tree Theatre, Richmond).

**Bethany Wells** | Designer

Productions at the Finborough Theatre include *Spokesong*.
A graduate of the Bartlett School of Architecture and the Royal College of Art, Bethany was awarded the Helen Hamlyn Design Award 2011 and was selected for the Wallpaper Graduate Directory 2012. Bethany has a choreographic, physical approach to performance design, with experience in designing for rural touring, installation, promenade and site-specific performance.
Recent performance design includes *It Burns It All Clean* (Selina Thompson at the West Yorkshire Playhouse), *In-finite Space* (IJAD Dance Company at the Vault Festival), *SOUTH* (Shred Productions at the Lowry Studio, Salford), *The Rage Receptacle* (Ellie Harrison, Grief Series at the West Yorkshire Playhouse), *Cat in Hell* (Junction Theatre, Cambridge). Work currently in development includes *Canterbury Tales* (Impulse Collective at the New Diorama Theatre), *The Unfair* (Ellie Harrison, Grief Series), *Impossible Lecture* (Beacons Festival) and *Other Acts of Public WARMTH*, a mobile sauna and performance venue (The Stables, Old Granada Studios). Bethany is a member of the Young Vic Performance and Ecology Network and is a Tamasha Developing Artist.

**Peter Harrison** | Lighting Designer

Productions at the Finborough Theatre include *Japes*, *The Very Nearly Love Life of My Friend Paul, Too True to Be Good* and *The White Carnation*. Trained at RADA. Theatre includes *Much Ado About Nothing* (Ludlow Festival), *All the Single Ladies* (Churchill Theatre, Bromley, and National Tour), *Britain's Got Bhangra* (Rifco Arts at Watford Palace Theatre), *The Doubtful Guest* (Hoipolloi at Theatre Royal Plymouth, and Watford Palace Theatre), *Wuthering Heights* (Tamasha Theatre Company at Lyric Theatre, Hammersmith), *Aladdin* and *Sleeping Beauty* (First Family Entertainment at Richmond Theatre), *Orestes* (Shared Experience) and *The Ballad of the Burning Star* and *Translunar Paradise* (Theatre Ad Infinitum). Opera includes *Paul Bunyan* (Welsh National Youth Opera), *Orpheus in the Underworld* (Royal College of Music) and *Carmen* (Hampstead Garden Opera). As an Associate Lighting Designer, work includes *The Commitments* (Palace Theatre), *I Can't Sing* (London Palladium), *Collaborators* (National Theatre) and *Written on Skin* (Festival d'Aix-en-Provence) with Jon Clark, *In a Minor Key* (Mikhailovsky Ballet, St. Petersburg) with Simon Bennison and *The Wolves in the Walls* (National Theatre of Scotland) with Natasha Chivers.

**Max Pappenheim** | Composer and Sound Designer

Productions at the Finborough Theatre include Sound Designer and Composition for *Martine, Almost Near, Variation on A Theme*, *The Hard Man, Black Jesus*, *Summer Day's Dream*, *The Hospital at the Time of the Revolution*, *Somersaults*, *The Soft of Her Palm and The Fear of Breathing*. He directed *Perchance to Dream*, *Nothing is the End of the World (Except for the End of the World)* which was nominated for three OffWestEnd Awards, and *Dream of Perfect Sleep*.

Other Sound Design and Composition includes *The Hotel Plays* (Defibrillator at the Langham Hotel), *Fiji Land*, *Our Ajax* (Southwark Playhouse), *Mrs Lowry and Son* (Trafalgar Studios), *CommonWealth* (Almeida Theatre), *Being Tommy Cooper* (National Tour), *Irma Vep*, *Borderland*, *Kafka v Kafka* (Brockley Jack Studio Theatre), *Four Corners One Heart* (Theatre503), *Freefall* (New Wimbledon Theatre Studio) and *Below the Belt* (Edinburgh Festival). As Associate, *The Island* (The Young Vic). Max was nominated for an OffWestEnd Award 2012 for Best Sound Designer.

**Sunday/Monday/Tuesday Productions at the Finborough Theatre**

The Finborough Theatre is committed to its multi-award-winning artistic policy of presenting both plays and music theatre, concentrated exclusively on vibrant new writing and unique rediscoveries of neglected work from the 19th and 20th centuries. Our Sunday/Monday/Tuesday productions (nine performances on Sunday and Monday evenings and Tuesday matinees, playing over a three-week period, in repertoire with our main show) allow us to produce even more work that we believe deserves to be seen – often directed by exciting emerging directors. Sunday/Monday/Tuesday productions are performed on the set and with the lighting rig of our main show.

# FINBOROUGH | THEATRE
## VIBRANT **NEW WRITING** | UNIQUE **REDISCOVERIES**

"A disproportionately valuable component of the London theatre ecology. Its programme combines new writing and revivals, in selections intelligent and audacious." *Financial Times*

"The tiny but mighty Finborough… one of the best batting averages of any London company." Ben Brantley, *The New York Times*

"The Finborough Theatre, under the artistic direction of Neil McPherson, has been earning a place on the must-visit list with its eclectic, smartly curated slate of new works and neglected masterpieces." *Vogue*

Founded in 1980, the multi-award-winning Finborough Theatre presents plays and music theatre, concentrated exclusively on vibrant new writing and unique rediscoveries from the 19th and 20th centuries. Behind the scenes, we continue to discover and develop a new generation of theatre makers – through our Literary team, and our programmes for both interns and Resident Assistant Directors.

Despite remaining completely unsubsidised, the Finborough Theatre has an unparalleled track record of attracting the finest creative talent who go on to become leading voices in British theatre. Under Artistic Director Neil McPherson, it has discovered some of the UK's most exciting new playwrights including Laura Wade, James Graham, Mike Bartlett, Sarah Grochala, Jack Thorne, Simon Vinnicombe, Alexandra Wood, Al Smith, Nicholas de Jongh and Anders Lustgarten; and directors including Blanche McIntyre.

Artists working at the theatre in the 1980s included Clive Barker, Rory Bremner, Nica Burns, Kathy Burke, Ken Campbell, Jane Horrocks and Claire Dowie. In the 1990s, the Finborough Theatre first became known for new writing including Naomi Wallace's first play *The War Boys*; Rachel Weisz in David Farr's *Neville Southall's Washbag*; four plays by Anthony Neilson including *Penetrator* and *The Censor*, both of which transferred to the Royal Court Theatre; and new plays by Richard Bean, Lucinda Coxon, David Eldridge, Tony Marchant and Mark Ravenhill. New writing development included the premieres of modern classics such as Mark Ravenhill's *Shopping and F\*\*\*ing*, Conor McPherson's *This Lime Tree Bower*, Naomi Wallace's *Slaughter City* and Martin McDonagh's *The Pillowman*.

Since 2000, new British plays have included Laura Wade's London debut *Young Emma*, commissioned for the Finborough Theatre; two one-woman shows by Miranda Hart; James Graham's *Albert's Boy* with Victor Spinetti; Sarah Grochala's *S27*; Peter Nichols' *Lingua Franca*, which transferred Off-Broadway; and West End transfers for Joy Wilkinson's *Fair*; Nicholas de Jongh's *Plague Over England*; and Jack Thorne's *Fanny and Faggot*. The late Miriam Karlin made her last stage appearance in *Many Roads to Paradise* in 2008. UK premieres of foreign plays have included Brad Fraser's *Wolfboy*; Lanford Wilson's *Sympathetic Magic*; Larry Kramer's *The Destiny of Me*; Tennessee Williams' *Something Cloudy, Something Clear*; the English premiere of Robert McLellan's Scots language classic, *Jamie the Saxt*; and three West End transfers – Frank McGuinness' *Gates of Gold* with William Gaunt and John Bennett; Joe DiPietro's *F\*\*\*ing Men*; and Craig Higginson's *Dream of the Dog* with Dame Janet Suzman.

Rediscoveries of neglected work – most commissioned by the Finborough Theatre – have included the first London revivals of Rolf Hochhuth's *Soldiers* and *The Representative*; both parts of Keith Dewhurst's *Lark Rise to Candleford*; *The Women's War*, an evening of original suffragette plays; *Etta Jenks* with Clarke Peters and Daniela Nardini; Noël Coward's first play, *The Rat Trap*; Charles Wood's *Jingo* with Susannah Harker; Emlyn Williams' *Accolade*; Lennox Robinson's *Drama at Inish* with Celia Imrie and Paul O'Grady; John Van Druten's *London Wall* which transferred to St James' Theatre; and J. B. Priestley's *Cornelius* which transferred to a sell out Off Broadway run in New York City.

Music Theatre has included the new (premieres from Grant Olding, Charles Miller, Michael John LaChuisa, Adam Guettel, Andrew Lippa, Paul Scott Goodman, and Adam Gwon's *Ordinary Days* which transferred to the West End) and the old (the UK premiere of Rodgers and Hammerstein's *State Fair* which also transferred to the West End), and the acclaimed 'Celebrating British Music Theatre' series, reviving forgotten British musicals.

The Finborough Theatre won *The Stage* Fringe Theatre of the Year Award in 2011, *London Theatre Reviews'* Empty Space Peter Brook Award in 2010 and 2012, the Empty Space Peter Brook Award's Dan Crawford Pub Theatre Award in 2005 and 2008, the Empty Space Peter Brook Mark Marvin Award in 2004, and swept the board with eight awards at the 2012 OffWestEnd Awards including Best Artistic Director and Best Director for the second year running. *Accolade* was named Best Fringe Show of 2011 by *Time Out*. It is the only unsubsidised theatre ever to be awarded the Pearson Playwriting Award (now the Channel 4 Playwrights Scheme) nine times. Three bursary holders (Laura Wade, James Graham and Anders Lustgarten) have also won the Catherine Johnson Award for Pearson Best Play.

## www.finboroughtheatre.co.uk

The Finborough Theatre has the support of the Channel 4 Playwrights' Scheme, sponsored by Channel 4 Television and supported by The Peggy Ramsay Foundation

The Finborough Theatre is a member of the Independent Theatre Council, Musical Theatre Network UK and The Earl's Court Society www.earlscourtsociety.org.uk

**Mailing**
Email admin@finboroughtheatre.co.uk or give your details to our Box Office staff to join our free email list. If you would like to be sent a free season leaflet every three months, just include your postal address and postcode

**Follow Us Online**

  www.facebook.com/FinboroughTheatre
www.twitter.com/finborough

**Feedback**
We welcome your comments, complaints and suggestions. Write to Finborough Theatre, 118 Finborough Road, London SW10 9ED or email us at admin@finboroughtheatre.co.uk

**Playscripts**
Many of the Finborough Theatre's plays have been published and are on sale from our website.

**Finborough Theatre T-Shirts are now on sale from the Box Office, available in Small and Medium £7.00.**

Smoking is not permitted in the auditorium and the use of cameras and recording equipment is strictly prohibited.

In accordance with the requirements of the Royal Borough of Kensington and Chelsea:

1. The public may leave at the end of the performance by all doors and such doors must at that time be kept open.

2. All gangways, corridors, staircases and external passageways intended for exit shall be left entirely free from obstruction whether permanent or temporary.

3. Persons shall not be permitted to stand or sit in any of the gangways intercepting the seating or to sit in any of the other gangways.

The Finborough Theatre is licensed by the Royal Borough of Kensington and Chelsea to The Steam Industry, a registered charity and a company limited by guarantee. Registered in England and Wales no. 3448268. Registered Charity no. 1071304. Registered Office: 118 Finborough Road, London SW10 9ED.

The Steam Industry is under the overall Artistic Direction of Phil Willmott. www.philwillmott.co.uk

## Friends

The Finborough Theatre is a registered charity. We receive no public funding, and rely solely on the support of our audiences. Please do consider supporting us by becoming a member of our Friends of the Finborough Theatre scheme. There are four categories of Friends, each offering a wide range of benefits.

**Brandon Thomas Friends** – David and Melanie Alpers. The Beryls. Penelope H. Bridgers. David Day. Mike Frohlich. Bill Hornby. Barbara Marker. Barbara Naughton. Sally Posgate. Michael Rangos. Nick Salaman. Barry Serjent.

**Richard Tauber Friends** – Val Bond. James Brown. Tom Erhardt. Bill Hornby. Richard Jackson. Mike Lewendon. John Lawson. Harry MacAuslan. Mark and Susan Nichols. Sarah Thomas.

**Lionel Monckton Friends** – S. Harper. Philip G Hooker. Martin and Wendy Kramer. Deborah Milner. Maxine and Eric Reynolds.

**William Terriss Friends** – Stuart Ffoulkes. Leo and Janet Liebster. Peter Lobl. Paul and Lindsay Kennedy. Corinne Rooney. Jon and NoraLee Sedmak.

*In loving memory of James Garnett, 1930 - 2013*

Dameon Garnett

# 17

OBERON BOOKS
LONDON

WWW.OBERONBOOKS.COM

First published in 2014 by Oberon Books Ltd
521 Caledonian Road, London N7 9RH
Tel: +44 (0) 20 7607 3637 / Fax: +44 (0) 20 7607 3629
e-mail: info@oberonbooks.com
www.oberonbooks.com

A catalogue record for this book is available from the British
Library.

PB ISBN: 978-1-78319-158-1
E ISBN: 978-1-78319-657-9

Visit www.oberonbooks.com to read more about all our books
and to buy them. You will also find features, author interviews and
news of any author events, and you can sign up for e-newsletters
so that you're always first to hear about our new releases.

# Characters

SCOTT (17)

LISA (34)

DANIEL (late 30s)

LEO (15/16)

The set consists of a kitchen, centre stage, and bunk beds to the left, making up the boys' bedroom.

# Act One

*Friday evening. A Liverpool couple, LISA and DANIEL, are in their kitchen, preparing a meal. There is a table and chairs. LISA is breathless and nervous; DANIEL gives her a reassuring squeeze, or embrace. She drops a fork.*

LISA: Damn.

*DANIEL picks it up. Pause as they look at each other.*

DANIEL: Take it easy.

LISA: Yeh.

*Pause. They carry on.*

DANIEL: It's fine.

*Silence as they continue to prepare.*

LISA: Shall I do the table?

DANIEL: Go 'ead then.

*LISA does so but cannot make up her mind how to set it out.*

LISA: *(Trying different arrangements.)* Maybe…I dunno.

*She re-arranges it.*

Do ya think…which side should we sit him on?

DANIEL: I don't think he cares.

LISA: Maybe I should sit next to…

*Pause.*

I hope it's gonna be all right. I hope…

DANIEL: Take it easy. Getting worked up over nothing.

LISA: Nothing?

DANIEL: You know what I mean.

LISA: Not really.

DANIEL: Lisa…

*He goes over to her. They hold hands and look at each other.*

LISA: And what about the…you know…the ashes; where the hell could they have got to? It's driving me crazy.

DANIEL: They'll turn up. Anyway, it's nearly ready. Do you wanna give him a shout?

LISA: Yeh. I'll just finish…

*She finishes setting the table as DANIEL lays out the food. LISA goes off stage right and shouts up.*

Scott! Scotty – ya tea's ready! Come on down lad.

DANIEL: *(Making fun of her.)* 'Come on down'…

LISA: What?

*Eventually a 17-year-old boy, SCOTT, enters. He wears a hooded top and is carrying a small tank with a towel over it. There is a book on top of the tank.*

LISA: All right lad?

DANIEL: Sit down mate.

*He puts the tank down in the corner.*

LISA: What's that?

SCOTT: *Dr Who.*

LISA: What – in that thing?

SCOTT: No – I mean me book.

LISA: Gonna say…

DANIEL: She's pulling ya leg Scott. She meant the box. What's in it?

*Pause.*

LISA: Have you gotta nice big cake in there for us?

SCOTT: Wha'?

LISA: Never mind.

*Silence as DANIEL puts the dinner out. SCOTT does not look impressed. DANIEL sits down and both he and LISA look on at him, relishing and expecting a challenge.*

DANIEL: Well?

LISA: Try it.

*They start eating, SCOTT tentatively.*

SCOTT: *(After a pause.)* What is it?

LISA: Mushroom risotto.

SCOTT: *(Playing with it.)* Wha' – like, rice an' stuff?

LISA: Yeh. It's rice. Nice rice. Try it.

*Pause. SCOTT takes a mouthful.*

SCOTT: Can I 'ave chips?

*DANIEL looks at LISA.*

LISA: No…remember what we said…you're gonna…just give it a go. It's nice.

SCOTT: I always 'ave chips on a Fridee.

LISA: You 'ave chips every day…used to…

DANIEL: Go easy…

*Pause.*

Look, Scotty, I love chips too. But we can't have chips all the time now, can we?

SCOTT: Why not?

LISA: They make you sick.

*Pause.*

SCOTT: I've never been sick from eatin' chips.

LISA: I mean…it's not…they're not good for you…all the time. You'll get scurvy.

SCOTT: Wha'?

LISA: Remember. You're gonna try and eat more like what we do...remember?

*SCOTT eats more risotto.*

SCOTT: I don't like mushrooms.

LISA: They're only small ones.

SCOTT: Mushrooms are poisonous.

LISA: Not these ones.

SCOTT: How do ya know?

LISA: They're from Marks and Spencer. Go on – try some.

*He does so. Silence.*

SCOTT: I can make chips meself.

DANIEL: Can ya? That's handy...handy to know, eh Lis'. Tell ya what...next time we make chips, you can be in charge, eh Lisa...can't he?

*Silence as SCOTT attempts to plough on through the meal. LISA is pleased that he is having a go.*

SCOTT: Where's Leo?

DANIEL: Gone to his nan's mate. He sometimes goes on a Friday.

SCOTT: Where does she live?

DANIEL: Maghull.

*Pause.*

SCOTT: Can I go?

DANIEL: What...now?

SCOTT: No I meant...some time...

DANIEL: Yeh...yeh...sure. She wants to meet ya. Told 'er all about you.

*Pause as they carry on eating.*

LISA: Got a treat for you Scotty…if you eat it all up.

DANIEL: He's not a baby.

LISA: He is…

DANIEL: Lisa!…he's a man now, aren't ya lad?

LISA: Do you like Viennetta slice Scott?

SCOTT: 'Ave ya got any ice-cream?

LISA: It is ice-cream.

DANIEL: I've gotta an even bigger surprise for him, next week.

LISA: What?

DANIEL: How about…I was thinking…Scott, right, I'll take you down to our Leo's school, next week, right. Get you enrolled. They've got a really good sixth-form there.

LISA: Not now Daniel…

DANIEL: Why not…I'm just saying…be a nice little drive for you as well, in the new Mondeo…

LISA: Oh don't start that – him and his new bloody car – he loves that car more than he does us…

*SCOTT throws up on to his plate. Silence.*

DANIEL: Oh…okay…erm…

*DANIEL quickly takes the plate away.*

LISA: Put it in the bin.

DANIEL: What – the plate?

LISA: No – ya divvy…you know… *(To SCOTT.)* you all right lad?

SCOTT: Yeh. Sorry.

LISA: It's okay…I just wanted you to…

*Pause.*

Make him some chips Dan'.

DANIEL: Yeh sure…in a minute.

SCOTT: Sick.

LISA: What – not again?

SCOTT: No – I mean, sick…about the chips…

LISA: Oh…

*Pause. SCOTT goes to the towel-covered tank and picks it up. He brings it over to the table and sits down with it on his lap.*

SCOTT: I want ya to meet Dave.

LISA: Dave? Is that ya mate from school?

SCOTT: No – Dave.

*He removes the towel from the tank and lifts out a snake. LISA jumps up.*

LISA: Fucking Jesus tonight! – get it out of here – it's a fucking snake – Daniel – he's got a fucking snake! Get it out!

SCOTT: He doesn't bite.

DANIEL: Right…

LISA: Get it out Daniel!

SCOTT: It's okay. He doesn't eat much.

LISA: Oh Jesus…Did you know he had that thing upstairs!?

DANIEL: No!

LISA: How long…I never knew he had that upstairs!

SCOTT: He just eats what I eat. I've been feedin' him salt an' vinegar crisps. I 'aven't 'ad time to get down the pet shop.

LISA: What for?

SCOTT: To get him his like proper food.

DANIEL: Like what?

LISA: Mammals!

SCOTT: Mice.

LISA: Told ya. Jesus.

SCOTT: It's okay. They're already dead. You just put them in the freezer.

LISA: You what?

SCOTT: An' then let them go soft again, before he eats them.

LISA: Scott – listen – I can't have a snake in the house…

SCOTT: He's me best mate – *(To the snake.)* aren't ya Dave?
Where ever I go – 'e goes…an' where ever 'e goes, I go…

LISA: Where's that – Chester Zoo? Look, Scott…

DANIEL: You should keep Dave in your room Scott.

LISA: 'Keep Dave in your room'…who are you all of a
sudden…Dr fucking Dolittle? He can't keep it anywhere! I
want it out of here Daniel…now!

DANIEL: Oh come on Lisa…

LISA: Come on what?!

DANIEL: It's only tiny…

SCOTT: Like them mushrooms.

LISA: What?!

DANIEL: As long as he keeps it in the tank…

LISA: Are you for real?

DANIEL: Why not?

LISA: Daniel!

SCOTT: I look after him.

DANIEL: Come on Lis' – it's called Dave…

LISA: So?

DANIEL: It can't be dangerous…you don't get dangerous
snakes called Dave…look at the size of it…

SCOTT: He's a corn snake…

LISA: So. It's not vegetarian, is it?

DANIEL: Yeh but…Dave's such a cool name…

LISA: I don't care if it's called Tiny Tears…by the time it's
    finished with them frigging mice…you don't know how big
    it's gonna get!

DANIEL: Don't talk soft.

SCOTT: The' don't get any bigger than this.

DANIEL: Maybe if you put Dave back in the box Scott?

SCOTT: It's a tank.

LISA: Can it get out?

SCOTT: No. The holes are too small. Only if I open the lid.

LISA: 'Open the lid'…

    *SCOTT puts DAVE back in his tank.*

DANIEL: There you go.

LISA: Jesus.

DANIEL: All safe now.

    *Pause.*

LISA: Scott, do us a favour lad, next time you wanna introduce
    me to a pal…can it not be a snake?

    *Pause.*

SCOTT: Can I have me chips now?

    *Fade.*

## SCENE 2

*The same evening. We hear the 'Dr Who' theme tune. Lights up on SCOTT
in his bedroom, watching a clip of the very same on his laptop. He sits
on the bottom of two bunk-beds, Dave by his feet, in his tank. There is
a framed picture of Scott with his mother on a side table. From the top*

*bunk hangs a very pristine school uniform, belonging to LEO. The top bed has a Liverpool FC duvet cover, the bottom one, 'Thomas the Tank Engine'. Enter LEO, aged 15, wearing pyjamas. He is slightly built and young-looking, even for his age. SCOTT closes his laptop and picks up his Dr Who book. The two boys stare at each other.*

SCOTT: What are they?

LEO: Pyjamas. *(He has a Liverpool accent like SCOTT, though more middle-class.)*

SCOTT: You look special.

LEO: What do you wear in bed?

SCOTT: Me undies. Unless it's too hot.

*LEO stares at the tank.*

SCOTT: I told you – he can't get out, an' if he did…he's harmless.

*Pause.*

Look, I'll put him in the spare room, when it's warmer.

LEO: What does it eat?

SCOTT: Children.

*LEO climbs up on to the top bunk; starts to play a computer game.*

SCOTT: *(Referring to the duvet cover.)* Why do I have to have Thomas the tank engine?

LEO: Oh, it's because you don't like football. Remember you said. Mum didn't know what to get you.

SCOTT: Right, so everyone who doesn't like footy, must like Thomas the tank engine?

LEO: It's an old one o' mine.

SCOTT: Great. At least it's not Harry Potter. Then I would have to burn it.

*LEO leans over.*

Jokes. Anyway, give us a pillow, ya little German. I've only got one. You've got loads up there – the Sultan of Dhubi.

*LEO leans over and throws a pillow down.*

Tar.

LEO: I hate Harry Potter as well.

SCOTT: *(Standing up.)* Put it there mate.

*They shake hands.*

SCOTT: How come there's all that gear in the hall?

LEO: What gear?

SCOTT: Looks like a tent and stuff.

LEO: Oh yeh. I was gonna go camping with my mate, Mally. We was gonna kill frogs.

SCOTT: Why didn't ya go?

LEO: Your mum died. I mean the other…one…

*Pause.*

SCOTT: You shouldn't kill frogs.

LEO: Why not?

SCOTT: It's bad luck…especially for the frogs. Plus…you get nightmares.

LEO: How do you know?

SCOTT: This Irish fella wrote a poem abou' it. I read it in English. It's proper scary.

*Pause.*

Are you good at camping?

LEO: Yeh. I go every year.

SCOTT: How come you're scared o' snakes then?

LEO: The' don't have snakes in the Delamere Forest. It's not the Congo.

SCOTT: That's what you think. I could show you how to start a fire.

LEO: So could I – if I had a match and some petrol.

SCOTT: Funny.

LEO: Anyway, I can set up a tent, quicker than my dad now. I'm good at DT as well.

SCOTT: What's that?

LEO: Design Technology.

SCOTT: Wood work?

LEO: Got my own tool kit. I've got like, loads o' screw-drivers.

SCOTT: I wanna go to Marbella.

LEO: Where's that?

SCOTT: In Spain.

LEO: Do you wanna come camping with us?

SCOTT: Might do...I'll probably be in Spain by then though.

LEO: Why do you wanna go there?

*Pause. LEO goes back to his game. SCOTT, checking LEO is not looking, pulls out the wooden box containing his mother's ashes from under the bed; it is well concealed in two bags. He holds it and looks at it; shakes it, then listens to it. LEO gently nudges SCOTT with his foot, who puts the box away immediately.*

LEO: Can we swap beds?

SCOTT: Why?

LEO: Then you wouldn't have to have Thomas the tank engine.

SCOTT: He's growing on me. Thanks for being so considerate though.

LEO: Oh go on. I can't sleep up here.

SCOTT: Why not?

LEO: Scared o' heights.

SCOTT: What about Dave?

LEO: You said you were gonna move him.

SCOTT: Not yet.

LEO: I hate bunk-beds. It's only cause me mum wants to keep the spare room for her aerobics. Wouldn't mind, she's still got a really fat arse.

SCOTT: I'm the oldest anyway. I'm entitled to the bottom bunk.

LEO: It's my room.

SCOTT: Sorry. I didn't want me mum to die.

LEO: I never meant it like…they have bunk beds in prisons.

SCOTT: Look, if you can cope with camping, you can cope with a top bunk.

LEO: Please Scott…I'll give you my best screw-driver…

SCOTT: I don't need a screw-driver.

LEO: You never know when you might need one.

SCOTT: I'm okay thanks.

LEO: I need better access to my school books, to do my homework. I'll wake you up…I go the toilet during the night… every night…

SCOTT: I'll live with it.

LEO: I might have an accident – might accidentally wee on your face.

SCOTT: I'm open to new experiences.

LEO: Or worse…

SCOTT: Still keeping an open-mind.

LEO: Go on.

SCOTT: No. I'm bigger than you!

LEO: So.

SCOTT: I'm not designed for a top bed. Look at you...half boy, half quaver...if you fall out...you're guaranteed a safe landing – I'd break in to little pieces...on impact.

LEO: Swap.

SCOTT: No! Stop asking me.

*Enter LISA, wearing slippers with over-large bunny-rabbit heads.*

LISA: What are youse two up to, eh?

LEO: When can Scott have the spare room?

LISA: Don't start. I've got ya these lovely bunk beds.

LEO: He doesn't like Thomas the tank engine.

LISA: Sorry Scott – I meant to pick you up a new cover today. You can come with us tomorrow, can't ya...pick one yourself. We might find one with a snake on it.

LEO: Snakes eat rabbits. I can't sleep in a bunk. I told you.

LISA: Why not?

LEO: It's effectin' my revision. I'm knackered. I keep passing out when I try to read anything *(He demonstrates.)* I'm gonna fail my mocks.

LISA: Don't say that Leo. You'll get use to it.

LEO: I won't. Scott doesn't wanna share a room neither.

SCOTT: I don't mind.

LISA: We'll sort something out...eventually...it's fine for now.

LEO: You never do any exercise in there anyway.

LISA: Shut it you. I do do me exercises.

LEO: You look just the same.

LISA: You'll get a crack.

LEO: Sorry.

LISA: It's not all about losing weight.

LEO: What's it about then?

LISA: Heart rate...blood pressure...blood sugar......

LEO: So why don't you stop buying them – what are they called – French fancies?

LISA: That's the point...I need to do me exercise so I can have me little treats.

LEO: Little?

LISA: You be quiet...tryna show off in front o' Scott – making me look silly. You're turning into one gobby little get, going to that school.

LEO: Mum – I don't like sleeping on a top bunk bed – I feel stupid...Scott won't swap...

LISA: Scott's fine where he is...aren't you lad?

SCOTT: Yeh.

LISA: He's too old for the top bunk.

LEO: Why don't you move your exercise bike in to the shed, then there'd be room for a bed in the spare room?

LISA: You must be joking. That bike comes recommended by Davina McCall. It's got her signature on it. I'm not sticking that in the shed...

LEO: You never use it!

LISA: Eh – that's enough from you – Tom Brown's school days. I came in here to talk to Scott anyway. Shut your pie-hole *(Pause. To SCOTT.)* How is Dave getting on then...the lair of the white worm?

SCOTT: He's not a worm. He's a corn snake. An' he's not white.

LISA: I know. It's a story, about a snake.

SCOTT: I know. Read it at school.

LISA: All right. Calm down.

*Pause.*

Can I sit?

*No answer so she sits anyway.*

LISA: I just wondered…wondered, if you needed anything…
or Dave…

SCOTT: No.

LISA: What you reading?

SCOTT: Told ya…*Dr Who*…

LISA: I used to watch it. Which one…

SCOTT: *The City of Death.*

LISA: You like ya sc-fi, don't ya?

SCOTT: Suppose.

LISA: You got more books than DVDs. Not like him…

LEO: Shut up.

LISA: What's it about?

SCOTT: What?

LISA: What's it about – *The City of Death…*

*LEO starts pulling faces at SCOTT.*

SCOTT: It's about this alien with one eye and a very ugly
'ead – tryna steal the Mona Lisa from this big art gallery in
Paris.

LISA: The Louvre.

SCOTT: Yeh. Anyway he's got big plans. Do you really wanna
know?

LISA: Yes! I love Paris. You ever been?

SCOTT: No.

LISA: We took Leo last year. He loved it, didn't you Leo?

LEO: No.

LISA: We could take you there for your birthday…

SCOTT: You don't even know when it is…

LISA: Don't be daft!

*Pause.*

January the 16th.

SCOTT: Yeh.

*Pause.*

LISA: Anyway…just checking you're okay.

SCOTT: *(Turning more emphatically away from her.)* Whatever.

*She gets up to leave.*

LISA: You know…Scott…you know, you don't have to call me…you don't have to call me Lisa, you know…

SCOTT: What am I supposed to call you?

*Pause.*

LISA: It's a bloody tip in here…let's tidy it a bit…

*She goes to kneel down and reach under the bed.*

SCOTT: Leave it!

*Pause.*

I can unpack meself.

*Pause.*

LISA: Just checking you're okay.

*Fade.*

*Sunday. SCOTT is lying on his bed, now with a different duvet cover, listening to his iPod; something Spanish-themed coming out – the 'Lambada'. The noise is irritating LEO, perched on the top bunk, surrounded by school books and trying to revise. LEO adjusts his position to get comfortable, knocking some books on to the floor. SCOTT passes them back up then continues to listen to his music. Fade. Lights up on the kitchen, same time. DANIEL and LISA are in mid-flow, preparing dinner and moving things around quickly throughout the entire scene.*

DANIEL: I don't understand…why are you so…reluctant?

LISA: I'm not. I just think…he needs time, that's all.

DANIEL: You've got a diamond of a lad there Lis' – a diamond. He's bright.

LISA: Like his mum.

DANIEL: Look how much he reads.

LISA: I know.

DANIEL: So what's the problem? He just wasn't pushed at his old school, that's all.

LISA: He doesn't wanna go back to school.

DANIEL: I can understand…all that…what he had to go through…but…I'm telling you, school's the best place for him. The teacher said, he said, he can re-sit his exams, in the sixth-form.

LISA: Pass us that knife…

DANIEL: *(He does.)* I can get him enrolled first thing Monday.

LISA: Look, Daniel…I know you mean well…he just…he needs more time. He hasn't even…he hasn't got over it yet.

DANIEL: Lis' – he's not gonna get over anything sitting in his room all day. He needs something to do.

*LISA starts manically chopping food. Cut to SCOTT in his room, holding DAVE. LEO looks on, uneasy and unable to focus. Back to the kitchen.*

LISA: He needs to…he needs to face up to…certain things…
   otherwise, how can he concentrate on school work?

DANIEL: *(Sarcastically.)* Nice one Lis'…belter of an argument…

LISA: I did speak to him – I don't want him rushed in to
   anything.

DANIEL: You don't think he's good enough to go back to
   school…is that it? So, our Leo's gonna get an education…
   but Scott isn't?

LISA: Don't compare them!

DANIEL: So what's he gonna do with himself?

LISA: Daniel – you may have noticed, there's something going
   on.

   *Pause.*

   He didn't cry at the funeral – the next day the ashes
   mysteriously disappear – when he was supposed to scatter
   them.

DANIEL: They'll turn up.

LISA: Where? On the 82 bus? We can't exactly put adverts
   up round, can we? Missing box of ashes. Please return if
   found. I can't think where they've got to.

DANIEL: I told you. One of her family took them. They
   seemed a bit weird.

LISA: Weird? I'll tell you what's weird; Scott sitting up there
   stroking that snake – and Carol's ashes gone for a walk. It's
   like something from the Addam's family. We've got to find
   them.

DANIEL: That's exactly my point. We'll get him some
   counselling…at the school.

LISA: Nice one.

DANIEL: Every school has a counsellor. No biggee.

LISA: No – I don't like the sound of it.

DANIEL: Why not?

LISA: Who's gonna counsel the counsellor, after he's listened to our Scott? And then that poor sod'll need counselling as well. Vicious circle.

*LISA sits down. He goes over to her.*

Anyway, I just think…I don't think…I don't think he's ready, not for a school like that.

DANIEL: He is – he's a bright lad, trust me.

LISA: They might pick on him.

DANIEL: He just hasn't had…well…she didn't exactly push him, did she? I'll pay for extra lessons, if we need to.

LISA: I was thinking…maybe he could work for you…

DANIEL: Lisa – he's 17…he's got no qualifications…

LISA: I wish you wouldn't tell me how to bring up…

*Pause.*

Sorry.

*He rubs her shoulder and they clasp hands.*

LISA: Do you think he'll take Dave in to school?

DANIEL: No.

LISA: Anyway he's getting chips tonight; should bring a smile to his face.

*Continuous time, lights up again on SCOTT's room; he is back to listening to his iPod, now singing along to it; still something Spanish.*

LEO: Scott. Scott!

SCOTT: *(Taking his headphones out.)* Wapnin' lid?

LEO: You know, if you had your own room, you wouldn't need to use headphones.

SCOTT: So?

LEO: Well – shall I speak to my mum – see about getting you moved.

SCOTT: I'm okay.

LEO: Yeh. I know. *You're* okay.

SCOTT: Meaning?

LEO: This isn't working.

SCOTT: What's wrong?

LEO: I can't concentrate. You're too noisy. I can't use me desk, 'cause your stuffs all over it…I'm gonna fail me mocks, like…proper badly.

SCOTT: You're messier than me.

LEO: Yeh but – it's my mess.

SCOTT: Anyway I'm using me headphones, aren't I?

LEO: I can still hear it. I get it – you like Spain. I'm trying to revise for my physics you know…

SCOTT: Oh well…I'm really sorry it's my fault you're gonna fail your mocks, in your posh little school, so you won't be able to go to uni', with your posh little mates.

LEO: I only asked you to turn the music down.

SCOTT: No you didn't. You said you want me out.

LEO: I didn't say…

SCOTT: That's what you said.

LEO: So, what if I wanna pass my exams, anyway? I've got more chance of passing me exams, than you have of going to Spain…

SCOTT: That's what you think.

LEO: What else am I supposed to do? It's better than being a chav all your life.

SCOTT: Oh – so I'm a chav now?

LEO: I didn't mean you…

SCOTT: You called me a chav.

LEO: I didn't. You're being paranoid.

SCOTT: Yeh well – I get a bit like that, when people wanna kick me out of me room.

LEO: Your room? I've been here all my life!

SCOTT: Good for you.

LEO: How would you like it – if some stranger just turned up… with a snake?

*Pause.*

SCOTT: Suppose you've got a point.

LEO: Anyway, you snore.

SCOTT: I do not snore. That's unbelievable…you woke me up last night snoring!

LEO: I didn't!

SCOTT: How do you know? You were fast asleep?!

LEO: I can't get back to sleep…

SCOTT: You fart in your sleep.

LEO: So?

SCOTT: Little posh farts.

LEO: I can't help that…what do you want me to do…wake up and apologize? I bet you I don't anyway…

SCOTT: Okay I made that up. You do snore.

LEO: I don't! Right, when I woke up this morning…I was woken up, right…well…the bed was shaking.

*Pause.*

SCOTT: How do ya mean?

LEO: You know…I mean, the bed was shaking…

SCOTT: Oh – don't you accuse me o' that! Right, first night I slept here, right, in the middle o' the night – I tell you – you were at it lad – big time!

LEO: I wasn't!

SCOTT: Oh you were! I mean, I don't know how it's possible – you're built like a little whippet – but when you masturbate, the whole friggin' house shakes, never mind the bed frame. It was like sittin' on top o' the tumble dryer – when it's on its last cycle.

LEO: You're a liar! I wasn't doing that!

SCOTT: What were you doing then…polishing the crown jewels?

LEO: I don't…I wasn't…you're a liar Scott!

SCOTT: Yeh, yeh; I'm a big liar – bum's on fire. Anyway, as long as you use your own sock to do it in…fine by me.

LEO: You're disgusting…

SCOTT: Am I? Oh don't pretend…I don't mind…it's only natural, anyway. Just don't frighten Dave. He thought there was a tsunami coming, the other night. Maybe there was.

LEO: Scott…really…

SCOTT: Are you saying you don't…

LEO: None of your business.

SCOTT: If you can't get to sleep – it's a fantastic cure you know.

LEO: Not when I'm in the room thanks!

SCOTT: I'm talking about you.

LEO: Well don't!

SCOTT: Leo – don't pretend.

LEO: What?

SCOTT: You ought to be more careful with your laptop. Always delete your history.

*Pause.*

LEO: You didn't?

SCOTT: You said I could use it – yours is faster. Anyway it just came up, so to speak.

LEO: What did?

SCOTT: *(Smirking.)* Leather babes?! Really Leo – bit lightweight, isn't? You'd be better off just watching *Hollyoaks*. I was more impressed by milfhunter.com.

LEO: You're an arsehole!

SCOTT: As long as it's not your own mum.

LEO: What?!

SCOTT: And that website about bangin' ahl biddies in 'alf with fat boners – that was a bit messed-up, I thought.

LEO: What are you talking about!?

SCOTT: Okay I made that one up.

LEO: Don't use my laptop again. You're banned! I'm gonna put me password back on it.

SCOTT: Oh don't do that. Not the password! I'm only teasing ya.

LEO: Just leave it.

SCOTT: You can't exactly tell on me now can you – what are you gonna say? You'd have to admit to your ma that you're like…a hunter-gatherer of her best mates…

LEO: I don't…piss off Scott.

SCOTT: Do you like saggy tits then…

LEO: I'm not listening.

SCOTT: Fungus flaps…

LEO: Anyway you can't talk…

SCOTT: About what?

LEO: Mothers. Yours hasn't even been dead a week, and all you can do is make porn jokes.

SCOTT: Fuck off!

LEO: Why didn't you cry at her funeral Scott…is it because…

SCOTT: She's not dead!

*He lies on his bed, going in to a fetal position, facing the wall. Silence. LEO sits next to him, watching him. Opening lines of 'Chirpy Chirpy Cheep Cheep' – 'Where's your mother gone?'…fade; song leads into the next scene.*

## SCENE 4

*It is now Tuesday evening. DANIEL, SCOTT, LEO and LISA are in the kitchen, the latter pulling clothes out of shopping bags and holding them up against SCOTT. LEO plays on his game, occasionally looking up. The scene should be fairly fast-paced, to start with.*

LISA: *(Holding up an orange shirt against SCOTT's chest.)* That's a perfect fit that. It looks lovely on you. Go on – try it on.

SCOTT: No thanks.

LISA: Nice and summery.

SCOTT: It's autumn.

DANIEL: Not where we'll be taking you and Leo for your holidays.

SCOTT: *(Suddenly a little excited.)* Is it Spain?

LISA: Warm. But…no.

SCOTT: Oh.

LEO: With all these new clothes, he's gonna need that spare room.

LISA: You'll get a spare crack in a minute.

LEO: Like that statement makes sense.

SCOTT: How did ya get me measurements?

LISA: Your clothes don't wash themselves Scott. You get through them quickly enough.

DANIEL: Nowt wrong with that.

LISA: Never said there was.

DANIEL: I was just like you at your age Scott – never stopped washing and changing me clothes – once there's girls on the scene…eh…

LISA: Erm…we don't need to know about your past life… anyway don't be making assumptions.

*She pulls out another shirt from the bag…green…and puts it against SCOTT's chest.*

I thought you'd like this colour.

SCOTT: Why?

LISA: Snakes are green, aren't they?

LEO: Yeh but…not that green…

LISA: Well…this one is…

LEO: What green is that supposed to be?

DANIEL: Bit bright that Lis' – a health and safety hazard – like having your lights on full beam. We won't be able to look at him.

LISA: Shut it you minge bag…I paid for these anyway. I was thinking of getting something for Dave…but I was too scared to take his sizes.

DANIEL: Funny.

SCOTT: Where did you get them from?

LISA: Same place as I get all o' Leo's clothes…GAP.

LEO: *(Outraged.)* I don't get my clothes from there!

LISA: The ones I buy you are!

LEO: That's why I never wear them.

LISA: Cheecky get. David Beckham shops there now. It's on the posters. These are all GAP these.

*LEO audibly smirks. SCOTT looks at him.*

LEO: David Beckham does not shop at GAP!

LISA: Can't go wrong with GAP.

SCOTT: Great.

LEO: Can't go right either.

DANIEL: You shut up you – Gok-wan.

LISA: *(Referring to SCOTT's 'hoodie'.)* Come on take this off…try these on properly…

SCOTT: No.

*Pause.*

Me mum always let me choose me own clothes.

LISA: Well…I thought these would be nice for you…I mean these are perfect – *(Nodding at DANIEL.)* once we're on holiday…

SCOTT: Where's that gonna be…Thorpe Park?

LEO: The' won't tell me either Scott. It's probably the Harry Potter theme park. You won't get me and Scott going there mum…

LISA: You'll go where we take yis. Anyway it's not Harry Potters.

LEO: Potter.

LISA: It's not there – and I don't know what you're saying that for. You used to love reading his books.

LEO: I was like…10…

*SCOTT is getting visibly agitated.*

DANIEL: Let him try them on in his room Lis'…

LEO: My room.

SCOTT: I like wha' I'm already wearin'…

LISA: I know but…these'll make a nice change for you…

*(She tries to pull his 'hoodie' off him, as she pushes another shirt against him.)*

SCOTT: Leave it will ya!

*He grabs the shirt off her and throws it in to a corner, on to the floor.*

*Pause.*

I'm not wearin' this crap.

LISA: It's not crap Scott.

*Pause.*

I paid good money for these. Came out o' me own pocket.

*Pause.*

I was just thinking o' you.

*Pause.*

Perhaps I shouldn't o' bothered.

SCOTT: No.

*Pause.*

I wear me own clothes.

LISA: These are your clothes.

SCOTT: I don't want them.

LISA: Well they're yours now, anyway.

*Pause.*

You gonna pick that shirt up?

SCOTT: No.

*Pause.*

LISA: I think you should.

SCOTT: No thanks.

LISA: Pick it up!

*Pause.*

I went shopping for you. Now pick it up! Scott! Pick it up, I said!

SCOTT: I won't!

DANIEL: Go easy Lisa…I'll do it…

LISA: No! Leave it. Let him do it. I'm not 'aving this…

DANIEL: He doesn't like bright colours, that's all…

LISA: He doesn't like any colour him – the friggin' grim reaper – with his winter range! Look at him!

*Pause.*

DANIEL: *(Referring to the shirts.)* The' are a bit Bucks Fizz though, Lis'…a bit…*Miami Vice.*

LEO: I think they're disgusting.

LISA: Whose side are you two on?

LEO: Scott's.

LISA: Well you can buy his clothes for him then, out of your own pocket money, clever dick…

LEO: I was just saying.

LISA: Well don't! Now Scott, are you gonna pick that shirt up, because if you don't…

*LEO picks the shirt up and hands it to LISA.*

Put it down, I said…

LEO: Pick it up you said.

LISA: I'm gonna murder you in a minute lad…

DANIEL: Give it a rest Lisa…

LISA: I won't! I want him to pick it up!

SCOTT: I know what this is all about…

*Pause.*

LISA: What?

SCOTT: You know what! Leo knows as well, don't ya?

LEO: What?

SCOTT: When we were out yesterday. The lad from that school…saw me with Leo…'is that your brother…he looks like a chav'…it's only what Leo thinks o' me anyway…

LEO: I don't!

SCOTT: You used the word…

LEO: Not about you!

LISA: Leo doesn't think like that Scott.

SCOTT: Doesn't he?

LEO: He's been in a sulk about it all day. That lad's a dick Scott; everyone knows – forget about it.

DANIEL: Leo will always stand up for you Scott.

SCOTT: I'm not…so…so what if…I'm not dressing like one o'…and I'm not going to that school – and I'm not wearing these stupid clothes!

*He storms out. Pause.*

DANIEL: Good job we didn't show him the uniform.

*DANIEL helps LISA put the clothes back in the bags. LEO exits after SCOTT. 'The Lambada' plays again. Fade.*

*Wednesday morning. The boys' room. SCOTT and LEO are putting on their school uniforms. Eventually, SCOTT stands, looking very uncomfortable. His tie is deliberately knotted and positioned in a 'rebellious way'. LEO fixes it. Pause. SCOTT puts it back to 'rebellion style' again. LEO picks up his school bag.*

LEO: Come on – we better shoot. Bus leaves in ten minutes.

SCOTT: Is that a satchel?

LEO: Yeh. Why?

SCOTT: Jesus. Why don't you just have 'beat me up' – stitched on the side.

LEO: You're funny – with your Tesco's carrier bag.

SCOTT: Shows I've made no effort; whereas you – you've actually spent money, to look like a dweeb. Don't tell me – you're gonna put your mittens on next, the ones with the school crest on them. Did you sow your name badge on yourself?

LEO: No – the mitten fairy did it for me. I don't wanna be late for me first lesson. Come on.

SCOTT: Of course you don't.

LEO: It's Spanish you know – surely you can appreciate that. I'm already behind my work because o' you…

SCOTT: You go on…

LEO: What?

SCOTT: I'm not ready…I need to check on Dave – see if he's okay.

LEO: The bus driver doesn't know or care about Dave, Scott – if you don't get a move on, we're gonna miss it.

SCOTT: You go on…go on…off you go…go on without me.

LEO: You don't know the way.

SCOTT: I think I need a shower.

LEO: You've just had one.

SCOTT: Don't feel right. I need another one.

LEO: This is stupid…look, mum'll go mad if I don't take you with me.

SCOTT: I'm not your mascot. Look, just blame me anyway… say it was my fault…I had to…I had to go back for something…

LEO: Just come on…now…

SCOTT: I'm not going.

LEO: Why not?

SCOTT: I've got me reasons.

LEO: Reasons?

SCOTT: Yeh. Reasons.

LEO: I know what this is all about.

SCOTT: What?

LEO: All that stuff about… 'Leo called me a chav…Leo's ashamed of me'…blah, blah, blah…it's the other way round, isn't it? – you don't wanna be seen with me.

SCOTT: Bullshit.

LEO: I embarrass you – I'm not cool enough.

SCOTT: It's not your fault.

LEO: Look, if you're that bothered about my wearing my tie properly, I'll change it. See. *(He does so.)* But once we get to school, I'm putting it back. I've got my reputation to consider.

*SCOTT paces up and down, ripping off his tie.*

SCOTT: Look, I don't see why…I don't wanna go to your school. Right!

LEO: I'm not making you go. Don't get angry with me. Hurry up though 'cause me mum'll blame me…

SCOTT: Just leave it.

LEO: Get moving Scott!

SCOTT: You can't tell me what to do.

LEO: My room – my rules.

SCOTT: Fuck off!

LEO: I was joking. God. Look, come on…

SCOTT: I don't need to do this. I'm not like you. Look, I read – I don't sit there playing computer games all day…

LEO: So?

SCOTT: So – you're not interested in anything, not really…you just wanna, fit in – I don't need to go to school to prove to some… stuck-up twats, that I'm intelligent. I know I am. It's not about intelligence, anyway.

LEO: What's it about then – apart from missing the bus?

SCOTT: Yeh yeh – pass some shitty little GCSEs. Join the club. Jump through hoops.

LEO: So what are you gonna do today then? – buy a one-way ticket to Marbella?

SCOTT: I might just.

LEO: And where are you gonna get the money from?

SCOTT: We'll see.

LEO: I forgot…you're Dr Who, aren't you? – you can travel through space and time. You know Scott – I've only just like, noticed this, but…

SCOTT: What?

LEO: You're like…really immature. I feel sorry for you. Fine. I'm off to be part of the club, and jump through hoola hoops, or whatever…if you don't wanna come…that's up to you mate.

*LEO exits. SCOTT stands looking out after him.*

SCOTT: Leo…hang on…Leo…I'm coming…

*He exits after him. Fade.*

## SCENE 6

*The end of that same week; Friday. SCOTT, LEO, LISA and DANIEL sit at the kitchen table; it is the end of a meal. Silence. SCOTT pushes around some of the food he didn't eat. LISA starts to collect the plates in. She goes to pick up SCOTT's.*

DANIEL: Leave it!

LISA: What?

DANIEL: He can finish what we make him, for once.

*Pause.*

He's not Lord Muck.

LISA: I can't force him…

DANIEL: Does nothing I say count for anything in this house, any more?!

*Pause.*

LISA: *(To SCOTT.)* You gonna eat this?

SCOTT: No.

LEO: I will.

DANIEL: Leave it!

*Pause. LISA takes the plate away. DANIEL stands up suddenly, knocking some cutlery to the floor.*

DANIEL: For God's sake!

*Pause.*

At least he can clean up after his own tea!

LISA: Daniel?

DANIEL: Well – let him clean the dishes for a change…

LISA: No biggee.

SCOTT: I don't mind.

DANIEL: Good.

*Pause. LISA continues to clear up and SCOTT tries to help.*

DANIEL: *(To LISA.)* Sit down will you?

LISA: All right! Don't start.

LEO: I'll help. E are...

*DANIEL gives LEO a look. LEO helps SCOTT clear the dishes away. SCOTT is not sure what to do with his plate of unfinished food. Pause.*

SCOTT: Erm...shall I just put this in the sink?

DANIEL: Oh for God's sake!

*DANIEL storms up and takes the plate off SCOTT.*

You've had long enough to work it out...you can't be that...left-over food goes in the bin...what do you think we do it...put it on the floor and dance all over it?!

*DANIEL empties the plate in to a bin.*

LISA: Give him a break Daniel!

DANIEL: That's exactly what I tried to do!

*Pause.*

He knows what he's done – throws it right back in me face!

*Pause.*

How do you think it makes me feel? And our Leo.

LEO: I don't care.

DANIEL: Don't you be saying that – you!

LEO: Don't drag me in to this.

DANIEL: Have you two forgot – I'm chairman of the parents' committee?

LISA: We know.

DANIEL: They must think I'm...I am a laughing stock now. What's he going to do next – burn the school down?

*Pause.*

Here's me – I go in and persuade the Headmaster to take on a kid whose...he makes no effort!

LISA: *He* is in the room you know. I mean you can talk to his face.

DANIEL: Which one?

*Pause. LISA goes over to him.*

LISA: Kids do all kinds in his situation. I told you this. It could have been worse.

DANIEL: Could it? All right...let's ask him...why did you do it Scott?

*Pause.*

You made a fool out o' me! Leo's too embarrassed to go back to school.

LEO: Shut up dad! I never said that.

LISA: *(To SCOTT.)* Well? Come on.

*Pause.*

SCOTT: I said I'm sorry.

LISA: That's not an answer.

DANIEL: 'Cause he hasn't got one.

SCOTT: I 'ave!

*Pause.*

I was...I'm tryna save up.

DANIEL: What for? We're looking after you.

SCOTT: For Spain.

DANIEL: Spain?

SCOTT: Yeh.

*Pause.*

DANIEL: So – let me get this right – you went through all those kids' blazers – to get money, to go to Spain?

LISA: It wasn't every kid…

SCOTT: Yeh. Soon as I realized it was Leo's wallet…I put the money back.

LEO: Thanks Scott.

DANIEL: Oh great. What do you want – the Nobel Peace Prize? Okay, well done, apart from our Leo's – I told you – it was the entire class – watch the footage for yourself, if you don't believe me.

LISA: No thanks.

DANIEL: *(To SCOTT.)* Did you know I had to sit and watch every minute of it, with the Deputy Head?

*Pause.*

You must have realized…there'd be cameras everywhere?

*Pause.*

Obviously not. And what makes it worse – a big grin on his face, every time he finds a fiver! You'll give all that money back.

SCOTT: I already have.

DANIEL: And then I had to dispel the rumor about him walking round with a snake in his pocket!

*LEO laughs.*

LISA: Scott!

DANIEL: *(To LEO.)* What are you smirking for? Oh I haven't even had time to go in to that one! That's right. Pulling Dave out of his pocket – frightening the girls with it. *(Quoting himself.)* 'Oh don't worry Headmaster – Scott's a nice lad – his mum just passed away – a bit lost – but basically, a nice lad. Our Leo'll look after him'. Oh no – instead, he must be thinking, God knows, I've passed on to him…a cross between…Mowgli, and the Artful frigging Dodger. Walking round with a serpent in his pocket.

SCOTT: 'Is name's Dave.

DANIEL: That makes all the difference!

SCOTT: Anyway he's proper warm in me pocket. He's got crisps.

DANIEL: Jesus. What are you gonna do in Spain anyway? Sell castanets?

SCOTT: I'm goin' with me mate.

DANIEL: Oh yer – who's that – Billy frigging McGinty? In search of what exactly?

SCOTT: We're gonna get work.

DANIEL: Work? What work?

SCOTT: I don't know – yet. We're just gonna turn up, find some work…in the night-clubs.

DANIEL: That sounds like a well thought-out plan.

*(Slight pause.)*

About as well thought-out as your plan to steal money.

LEO: Forgot to tell you – nearly got full marks for my sustainable seating design.

DANIEL: *(To LISA.)* You never told me he was going to Spain.

LISA: I didn't know. He's not going anyway.

SCOTT: I am! When I get the dough together.

DANIEL: And how will you do that? Break in to Barclay's?

SCOTT: I dunno.

DANIEL: Exactly. And what about Dave? Is he going to? Got a feeling you might have a problem at customs mate, with that one.

SCOTT: We're gonna find work, that's all.

LISA: Don't be silly Scott.

DANIEL: In Spain?

SCOTT: Yeh. Why not? It's where everyone goes. I've seen it on Facebook.

DANIEL: Oh yeh – let me guess – everyone's having a big party, are they?

You see that's just it Scott…it's a party. Not real life. You must have heard it on the news.

SCOTT: What?

DANIEL: Spain's in an even worse crisis than we are.

LISA: Oh don't start…he's been reading the *Guardian* again. It all started in Starbucks.

DANIEL: And you haven't even got a qualification to your name.

SCOTT: You don't need GCSEs to do bar work.

DANIEL: Scott – people with degrees can't get proper…

SCOTT: Exactly – so what's the point?

DANIEL: You're an intelligent lad.

SCOTT: How do you know?

DANIEL: I can tell *(Pause.)* We got your old school reports. Look, you get yourself an education, you've got it for life… you can always go back to it.

LISA: *(To DANIEL.)* It's not like you've got a degree – money bags – and you've done all right. What are you qualified in? Key-stage 3 rock-climbing?

DANIEL: Thanks Lisa.

LISA: *(To SCOTT.)* Our Leo's gonna go to university.

LEO: If I can get my revision done…

LISA: What's good enough for him…good enough for you.

LEO: So why do I have to have the top bunk?

LISA: Shut it!

*Pause.*

SCOTT: Me mum

*Pause.*

She always lets me…she always lets me decide…what I wanna do.

*Pause.*

I am 17.

DANIEL: Yeh – and you're stealing money from your brother's wallet!

*SCOTT exits.*

LISA: Scott!

*Pause.*

You didn't have to say…you shouldn't have said that…

DANIEL: Excuse me…I've been at the school all day…having to explain everything…because Carol never set him any proper boundaries, apparently.

LISA: She's just died you insensitive bastard!

DANIEL: I'm sorry – Lisa!

*LISA exits. Pause.*

*(To LEO.)* What are you looking at – silent witness?

*LEO exits. Fade on kitchen. Continuous time. Lights up on LISA and SCOTT sitting on his bed in his room. Enter LEO.*

LISA: Get out you!

LEO: Sorry. Can I just get me history homework?

LISA: You'll be history – if you don't…hop it.

LEO: Knew you'd say that. I'm defo gonna fail, at this rate.

LISA: And I knew you were gonna say that an' all.

LEO: Liar. Bet you thought I was doing me Physics…

LISA: Is this physical enough for ya…

*She gets up to jokingly give him a boot with her rabbit-head slippers on.*

LEO: All right – I'm going.

*LEO exits.*

LISA: I know you'll take that money back.

SCOTT: I already 'ave.

LISA: You'll get suspended. Nothing worse, let's hope.

*Pause.*

Would it cheer you up – if I told you where we going on holiday?

SCOTT: I just wanna go to Spain.

LISA: Well…we're going to Nice anyway…it's not far from… did Carol used to take you to Spain?

SCOTT: Yeh. How do ya know?

LISA: Just a hunch.

SCOTT: Marbella. Yeh.

*Pause.*

LISA: Scott?

SCOTT: What?

LISA: We've…we've searched high and low, for her ashes, I mean, your mum's… ashes…I feel awful; like it's my fault. I tell you, when I find the bastard who's taken them…the stress we've been through.

*Pause.*

They'll turn up.

*LISA exits. Fade. Ominous sound of a coffin going into a furnace again; loud and disturbing, as if the whole auditorium is on fire. Spotlight on SCOTT sitting cross-legged in his room, with the box of ashes in front of him. He lights a match and watches it burn, then looks around the room. Fade.*

# Act Two

## SCENE 1

*A week later; Friday. DANIEL is in the boys' room setting up a desk for Scott next to the bunk beds. He is singing along to an old song playing from the radio, 'The Story of my Life', by Marty Robbins, hammering a nail here and there, working on the finishing touches. He looks over sheepishly at Dave's tank; talking to himself jokingly; 'All right – calm down Kaa. Easy. Don't be tempting me with no apples. I say you won't be tempting me. Made of iron me. Made of iron'. He knocks some nails on to the floor, 'Shit!'; then looks under the bed for them. Finding an unopened packet of condoms he stands up, laughs – thinks – puts them in his pocket. He goes back to looking under the bed for the nails and finds the bags containing the box of Carol's ashes. On taking the box out of the bags he sits on the bed and thinks. He hears SCOTT coming up the stairs then quickly puts the box back into the bags and pushes it under the bed. When SCOTT enters, dressed in his school uniform, he is picking up nails. SCOTT is carrying a school book.*

DANIEL: All right lad?

SCOTT: All right.

DANIEL: There you go mate – what do you think? *(Meaning the desk.)*

SCOTT: Thanks.

DANIEL: It's got draws an' everything…put a little lamp on there…you'll be able to do your studies properly now.

SCOTT: Yeh. Thanks.

*Pause.*

DANIEL: *(Leaning with his hand against the frame of the beds and looking at SCOTT.)* So – back in action now.

SCOTT: Yeh.

DANIEL: Going all right?

SCOTT: Yeh.

DANIEL: Good. Let me know…let me know if there's…any problems. You will tell me?

SCOTT: Of course.

DANIEL: Good.

*Pause.*

What are you up to now then?

SCOTT: Erm…I was just gonna read me book, you know, for English.

DANIEL: Oh yer. What you reading?

SCOTT: Some play by this dead gay bloke.

DANIEL: What you mean…he's very gay?

SCOTT: No – just dead. He used to be gay – now he's just dead.

DANIEL: Let's have a look.

*He takes the play off SCOTT and looks at it.*

DANIEL: *(Returning the book.)* Don't know that one. Anyway, pleased to hear you're getting back in to your studies now eh…no excuses, now you've got your desk…you'll be taking over our Leo soon.

*Pause.*

Listen Scott…erm, a little word…in you ear. Sit down lad.

*SCOTT sits on the bed and DANIEL sits next to him. He takes out the packet of condoms.*

Now listen…don't say anything. I found these. I want you to know…

SCOTT: Erm…

DANIEL: Don't say anything…you don't need to…I can guess what you're gonna say, anyway…I was young meself once, like you. Christ – I've just quoted Cat Stevens – anyway

– look – I just want you to know…girls, and an all that…I mean I'm assuming you like girls…

SCOTT: Yeh I do, but…

DANIEL: No buts…listen lad, I'm really glad you're taking precautions. I think that's great. But…look, I don't want you bringing any girls back here…okay?

SCOTT: Okay.

DANIEL: You see…our Leo…he's dead innocent. I'm not even sure he ever even thinks about sex. If he found these…he'd probably think they were party balloons, for his birthday…

*SCOTT smirks.*

Do you know what I'm saying? So, just keep these nice and hidden, eh? Do that for me, can't ya? Be careful.

*Pats him on the back and gives him the condoms.*

SCOTT: Sure.

DANIEL: Good lad.

*DANIEL stands. He pack his things away and goes to leave. Pause.*

DANIEL: No news on the ashes then?

SCOTT: I don't really watch the cricket.

DANIEL: I meant…your mum.

*Pause.*

SCOTT: No.

DANIEL: Everyone's been tryna locate them. Searching everywhere.

*Pause.*

Nothing?

SCOTT: Suppose not.

DANIEL: Shame.

*Enter LEO wearing his football kit and covered in mud.*

Jesus – smells like someone just slaughtered a lamb in here now.

LEO: What do you expect – been sweating like a pig, haven't I?

DANIEL: Lambs – pigs – bring in a cow – we'll have an entire farm-yard going on. Scott – any animals you wanna mention?

SCOTT: Erm…chickens?

DANIEL: Okay.

LEO: We won 2 nil.

DANIEL: Eh, I hope you're gonna get a shower before your tea…your mum's got something planned…

LEO: What's that? *(Pointing at the new desk.)* Is that for me birthday? I've already got a desk – I don't need two.

DANIEL: Erm – that's not for you, shine-a-light. You've got your new tent, haven't you? What more do you want? It's for Scott.

LEO: What?!

DANIEL: You were moaning about his stuff being on your desk.

LEO: Oh bleeding hell dad!

DANIEL: What?

LEO: You're joking, aren't you? Oh a great birthday this is turning out to be! There's no room. I can't concentrate on anything…me simultaneous equations are all over the place, 'cause o' this. I came third in Maths.

DANIEL: Eh – shut it you – Einstein. Remember what we said – we got a situation going on here…anyway, you'll be okay. You're a survivor.

LEO: What?

DANIEL: That's what I said.

LEO: Oh…look, dad…will you speak to my mum? I tried – I spoke to her the other day; she's not listening to me. She's just…not interested. There's no room in here, for both of us.

DANIEL: Enough, I said…

LEO: I'm not blaming Scott…no offence Scott…

SCOTT: None taken.

LEO: Can't you persuade me mum to stop pretending she's ever gonna use that room to get fit in?

DANIEL: Why don't you try telling her? And good luck by the way.

LEO: Tell her…I know!…tell her she's perfect as she is – you don't want her to change…

DANIEL: I could do without a slapped face right now.

LEO: This is a joke. On my birthday as well.

DANIEL: Oh diddums.

LEO: Thanks!

DANIEL: It's bad news. What are you gonna do – ring Childline?

LEO: I would – only me mum'll see it itemized on the phone bill; then the child-abuse'll really kick off.

DANIEL: Get washed, and stop moaning. See yis both in a bit.

*DANIEL exits.*

SCOTT: Happy birthday. Or is it merry Christmas?

LEO: Thanks. I need your help Scott. You've gotta get me mum to give you that room.

SCOTT: And you've gotta stop leaving certain things lying around.

LEO: Like what?

SCOTT: Like these.

*SCOTT pulls out the packet of condoms.*

LEO: Oh. Yeh.

SCOTT: I wonder why you really want this room to yourself. Are you bangin' some hottie? I understand, if you are.

LEO: Oh – don't be…it's not that. Well…

*Slight pause.*

It's a present – a joke – from Mally. You know. He was just, having a laugh. Standard.

SCOTT: I didn't find them anyway.

LEO: You what?

SCOTT: Your dad did.

LEO: What?

SCOTT: Yeh.

LEO: Shit.

SCOTT: I wouldn't worry about it. He thinks they're mine.

LEO: What? Didn't you tell him?

SCOTT: No. He'd have had a heart attack. He wouldn't have believed me anyway.

LEO: Oh thanks Scott. Put it there mate.

*They 'spud' each other. Pause.*

LEO: *(Completely changing his mood/tone.)* What do you mean he wouldn't have believed you?

SCOTT: Well…I know better…but, well…do you wanna know what he said?

LEO: What?

SCOTT: He said if you saw these, well, you'd probably think they were balloons for your party.

*SCOTT laughs.*

LEO: Did he now? Cheeky get. What would he know, anyway? He doesn't…shows you how much he knows…he's past it anyway.

SCOTT: Perhaps we should…

LEO: What?

SCOTT: Blow them up…as balloons…eh, be proper funny…if he thinks you're like…such a little kid…

LEO: I'm not. Can you?

SCOTT: What?

LEO: Blow them up?

SCOTT: Don't know – never tried.

LEO: *(Laughing.)* Get 'em out – let'see.

*They open the box, laughing.*

I've never seen one before.

SCOTT: Haven't ya?

LEO: Well…I mean, I have…not like these ones, probably…I mean.

*They take the condoms out of the box and play with them, giggling and laughing.*

They smell like…proper weird…

SCOTT: They're not called rubber jonnies for nottin'.

LEO: How big do they get?

SCOTT: Depends…I don't think it's just the condom that changes size. I've never used one.

LEO: Haven't you? I thought…

SCOTT: I meant…I can't remember, anyway…

LEO: Shall we try?

SCOTT: What – using one?

LEO: No divvie – blowing them up.

SCOTT: Go 'ead then. I will…

*He starts to inflate a condom. LEO rolls on the floor, laughing. SCOTT releases the air from the condom and it shoots up to the ceiling, making a noise. Both boys are now laughing uncontrollably. Continuous time: lights fade in the bedroom and come up on the kitchen – atmospheric/dim lighting. It is raining outside. We can hear the boys laughing from the kitchen. The kitchen table is set-up for LEO's sixteenth birthday; there are balloons, candles and novelty cups, etc. LISA is preparing the final touches.*

DANIEL: Just listen a minute, will you?

LISA: What now? Can't you see…

DANIEL: It'll only take…I think you should sit down, for this.

LISA: What? *(She stops, still holding a knife.)*

DANIEL: Put the knife down.

LISA: Why – I'm not gonna stab you! What have you done?

DANIEL: Not me – I haven't done anything.

LISA: Well?

DANIEL: It's Scott.

LISA: Scott? What about him? He's upstairs…

DANIEL: I know. Sit down.

LISA: All right! *(She sits.)* What's he done?

DANIEL: It's…the ashes…Carol's ashes.

LISA: What about them?

DANIEL: Scott's…Scott's got them.

*Pause.*

LISA: How do you know that?

DANIEL: I found them…under his bed. They're still there. I put them back…before…before, you know, he saw me.

LISA: When was this?

DANIEL: Just now.

LISA: How do you know…how do you know it's…the ashes?

DANIEL: What else could it be? It's a box of ashes!

LISA: I don't know.

DANIEL: It's not a box o' treasure, is it? He's not Long John Silver.

*Pause.*

LISA: Why – how has he got them?

*Pause.*

The little get…have you said anything to him?

DANIEL: No. Thought I'd speak to you first. He doesn't know I've found them.

LISA: Bloody hell.

DANIEL: I know.

LISA: What's he been playing at? All this time…

DANIEL: Search me.

LISA: *(Getting up.)* I'll bloody kill him…

DANIEL: Wait!

LISA: I'll kill him Daniel!

DANIEL: Hang on a minute…

LISA: What for? – he's had us going through all this bleedin' stress…

DANIEL: The party – remember…don't spoil it. Let's deal with this later.

LISA: Later? *(Slight pause.)* Why did you have to go and tell me about this now?

DANIEL: Because I've only just found out – soft girl.

LISA: It's put me right off me cake.

DANIEL: Take some deep breaths. Sit down…count to 10…

LISA: Frigg off Daniel. You're not the Dalai Lama.

DANIEL: I'm just saying…no point in spoiling Leo's birthday.

*Pause.*

Let's just…pretend everything's normal…right.

LISA: Bit difficult with the remains of a dead woman upstairs!

DANIEL: For now…for Leo's sake…let's just…pretend.

*Pause.*

We can deal with this later.

LISA: Certainly will.

DANIEL: Good. Right. Everything's normal…remember…let's just…act normal.

*She and DANIEL bring over some food from the kitchen tops, placing it on the table. LISA getting herself more and more angry inside as she thinks about SCOTT's deception – banging and slamming things down.*

*(Looking out of the window and referring to the neighbours.)*
I wish they'd pull the blinds down in that bloody conservatory. We don't all need to know what's going on next door.

DANIEL: Yeh.

LISA: Call them down will you?

DANIEL: *(Shouting.)* Leo – Scott – get down here! It's all ready.

*He sits down. There is a short interval where we can hear the sound of condoms being stretched, inflated, deflated, and the boys' laughter. DANIEL and LISA look at each other, confused. Eventually SCOTT enters; butter wouldn't melt, etc.*

Sit down Scott.

*He does so.*

Where's our Leo?

SCOTT: He's coming now.

LISA: *(Still moving things about.)* Happy with your new desk Scott?

SCOTT: Yes thanks.

LISA: Good. I'm glad you like it.

*Pause.*

You should have said 'thank you', before.

SCOTT: Oh sorry…I mean, erm, thanks. Thank you.

LISA: Better late than never.

*Pause.*

Have you got something to tell me lad?

DANIEL: Lisa!

SCOTT: What do you mean?

LISA: Let's get this out.

DANIEL: For God sake Lis' – not now.

LISA: Have you got something to tell me – about what you've got upstairs?

SCOTT: *(Looking around – looking at DANIEL for help.)* Is it about the condoms?

LISA: Condoms?

DANIEL: Oh no.

LISA: What's this about frigging condoms?

DANIEL: Nothing – Scott just – we were just having a laugh, that's all…there's nothing…

*Enter LEO, still muddy in his football kit.*

LISA: Leo – look at the state o' you!

LEO: What?

LISA: I thought your dad told you to get a shower.

DANIEL: I did. I did tell him. Don't blame me.

LEO: Sorry. I got distracted.

LISA: Who by? Bilbo Baggins?

LEO: Nobody.

LISA: You look like a dog's dinner. It's too late now. Just sit down will you. And put your party hats on!

*They all do so. Everybody is now sitting, glum, looking at each other and the floor, as LISA shuffles about.*

Right, I'm getting the cake out the fridge, so start being happy, now.

DANIEL: *(Doing as he is told and sitting up with a smile.)* Right – get ready to blow them candles Leo – big breaths now, eh…

*LISA places a birthday cake with candles on the table.*

Look at that…that looks fantastic, doesn't it Leo?

LEO: Sick! Thanks mum.

*LISA goes back to close the fridge door when something jumps out of it and runs across the kitchen floor. She screams her head off and jumps on to a chair.*

LISA: Jesus! What the fuck was that!? Oh my God!

DANIEL: What is it – what's wrong?

LISA: Something – oh fuck – something just legged it – out o' the fridge!

DANIEL: What?

LISA: I saw…it ran over there! Look…oh fucking hell!

DANIEL: What was it?

LISA: I don't know. A mouse or something. Jesus. What the hell – close all the doors – trap it in the room – how did it get in the fridge?!

DANIEL: It could be anywhere now – behind something.

*SCOTT looks down. DANIEL and LEO try to find the mouse; LEO whistling like a shepherd.*

LISA: *(Still on the chair.)* It's not a frigging sheep you idiot! Look in the fridge will you – there might be a whole army o' them in there!

DANIEL: Don't be daft.

*DANIEL goes over to the fridge. Pause.*

Shit.

LISA: What?

DANIEL: What – what's in that bag, on the bottom shelf?

LISA: What bag?

DANIEL: There! It's moving!

LISA: What!? You're joking…

DANIEL: *(Taking out the bag tentatively and peaking in to it.)* Oh my God…

LISA: What – what is it?

DANIEL: Mice – dead mice – one's still…

LISA: What?

DANIEL: I thought…one was, I thought one was still alive – it's – they're crawling with maggots. Eee! *(He drops the bag.)* That's why they're still moving – they're crawling with maggots…bloody hell. I can smell them.

LISA: *(Screaming.)* Get them out of here! Fucking now – get them out of here Daniel – now I said! Oh God!

DANIEL: All right – all right – I'll put them in the back yard.

LISA: No – out the front – down the street – I don't wanna see them – right down the street – get them out now!!

DANIEL: All right – all right!

LISA: Take them miles away I said!

*DANIEL runs out with the bag. LISA starts gagging up in to the kitchen sink. LEO and SCOTT sit in stony silence; LEO looking at SCOTT. Re-enter DANIEL.)*

DANIEL: Gone. I threw them right down the road.

LISA: I don't wanna see them!

DANIEL: It's all right. They'd have to have great navigational skills to find their way back here.

*LISA continues gagging in to the sink. She re-covers herself.*

LISA: We need to find that bastard mouse.

DANIEL: I know. It's running around somewhere, on fucking roller blades, I bet.

LISA: I don't fucking believe this. We'll have to scrub this place inside out. Everyone'll have to take a shower. We'll need a new fridge.

DANIEL: Eh?

LISA: All this food's gonna have to be chucked out. *(To SCOTT.)* What else have you got in that fridge – David Attenborough? You better have a very good explanation for this me ladeo! I tell you – you've burnt your bridges out with me, son shine, big time!

*Pause.*

LISA: Go on – explain yourself!

SCOTT: Erm…I got them for Dave…a lad in school…gave 'em to me; he knows where to catch 'em. Anyway…I thought the' were all dead. One must o' just been…stunned.

LISA: Not as stunned as I fucking was!

SCOTT: They're too big for Dave to eat…I was gonna chop 'em up, into smaller chunks…

LISA: *(Retching again.)* Oh God…

SCOTT: Put 'em in the freezer, later.

*LISA is retching up in the sink.*

I forgot. Sorry.

*Long pause.*

LISA: *(Re-covering herself.)* Well I hope you're happy. Everything's ruined. All this lovely food – I spent all day preparing this – it's all gonna have to be – chucked out... destroyed!

DANIEL: Not all of it...

LISA: It's all been in the fridge, hasn't it?! No-one's touching anything. Even the cake – that'll have to go...

LEO: I'll eat it mum.

LISA: No you fucking won't! They could have dropped out and got on to the cake...the' might be burrowing away inside it, right now...

DANIEL: They were well sealed, in that bag...

LISA: A fucking mouse just jumped out of it – dickhead! No-one's touching that cake – maggot city! *(Sitting down and crying.)* Oh fucking hell – why does everything for me have to be ruined – I spent all day preparing this as well – put me heart and soul in to it. It's all – ruined!

DANIEL: Come on now Lis'. We'll get a takeaway.

LISA: No – I won't be able to eat anything for an entire week. What next – maggots are gonna start turning up outside the house – in fucking taxis!

*(Crying.)* I just wanted things to be special – for me little boy on his birthday – why couldn't it be what I wanted. I'm so sorry son. I'm sorry.

*She hugs LEO. He indulges her but is embarrassed.*

Me innocent little lad. 16 now – and it's come to this – the house invaded by maggots; on his birthday as well! I'm sorry!

*She is tearful on LEO's a shoulder. At that moment a deflating condom comes flying in to the kitchen from the hallway, making a noise and landing on the table, near the cake.*

What the fuck's that now?

LEO: Erm…just a stray party balloon, I think, mum.

LISA: That frigging mouse had better not be taking flying lessons, in my house. What is it?

DANIEL: Just a balloon, babe.

*LISA picks up the condom.*

LISA: You know what this is – this is a…this is a… contraceptive.

DANIEL: No!?

LISA: What's it doing here?

*Pause.*

Daniel!

DANIEL: What?!

LISA: You know what? What was this stuff Scott said about frigging condoms, eh?

DANIEL: Oh – the lads were just joking, you know…

LISA: *(Standing.)* Right…I've had enough o' this…I want everything on the table…seeing as it already is – apart from that bleeding mouse…and, incidentally, no-one's going to bed tonight, until that thing's been hunted down, hung, drawn and quartered – not literally, Scott – Daniel, go upstairs and get – 'you know what'.

DANIEL: What?

LISA: You know what Daniel! Come on let's have everything out – the party's been ruined anyway. Go on then!

DANIEL: All right!

*DANIEL goes up to the boys room. LEO and SCOTT sit in silence staring at the table; LISA glaring at SCOTT. Re-enter DANIEL cradling an arm full of inflated condoms.*

LISA: What the hell are they?!

DANIEL: I thought you wanted…

LISA: Inflatable fucking condoms?! What's going on here? Do you all want me to have a nervous breakdown, or something?

DANIEL: Put everything on the table you said…

*A condom deflates and shoots up in to the air, hitting LISA in the face, if possible.*

LISA: Not these – eejut! *(To the boys.)* What the hell…what have you two been doing upstairs, eh? *(To DANIEL.)* Will you go and get that box?!

DANIEL: *(Realising.)* Oh! If you say so Lis'…

*He goes, dropping the inflated condoms on to the floor.*

SCOTT: *(Standing.)* Not Dave!

LISA: No not Dave; Dave – the snake…though if we set him loose he might be able to catch Geoffrey – the mouse…

*SCOTT listens anxiously as he hears DANIEL fumbling about in the room upstairs. LEO starts frantically popping the condoms; LISA joins in. DANIEL re-enters with the box containing Carol's ashes and puts it down in the middle of the table, next to the cake. Pause as SCOTT registers. LEO pops another condom.*

Stop that now you!

*Pause.*

Well? You better say something lad. You've had us all running round like blue-arse flies, looking for this, and all the time…go on. Say something? What are you playing at?

DANIEL: Go easy Lisa.

LISA: Never mind, go easy – I won't anyway. Go on! I'm not buying in to this little boy lost his mother stuff any more – I'm fed up of it. It was our Leo's birthday today – meant to be – I had a party planned – not much – but still, a little party – instead, I've ended up with a kitchen full o' maggots – I've got Norman Bates hiding his mother's body upstairs – and instead o' blowing out candles on me son's birthday cake, we're all standing round a box o' human remains! What the hell is going on?!

*Pause.*

Come on Scott – get talking!

*Pause.*

Speak to me – look at me I said! Will you wake…wake up – I'm your mother – not her!

*Silence.*

Your mother's looking at you. It's me – standing here, right now! I wasn't just a carrying case, you know. I gave birth to you! Me…I did. It's your mother, right here. Am I getting through to you? I want you to call me mum…call me mum, I said…

DANIEL: Lisa! You're not on girl…

LISA: Girl is right! 17 I was – how long do I have to keep paying for me mistake? It's been 17 frigging years an' all!

DANIEL: Lisa…

LISA: Oh for God's sake Daniel – it's not as if he doesn't know – she told him years ago. He knows who I am. We all do.

*Pause.*

Right, I tell you what, as everything's set up…let's celebrate, right now, shall we? The cake's ruined, but we've got the ashes. 17 candles on the ashes of my fucking life – right here – right now…here we go…

*She scoops up chunks of the cake with her hands and spreads it on top of the box of ashes, then starts to stick candles on to it.*

65

17 fucking candles right now…

DANIEL: Lisa – eh – stop it will you?!

LISA: We've got 16 all ready for Leo – we just need one more…

*She starts counting the candles. DANIEL tries to stop her but she pushes him away.*

DANIEL: Stop it Lisa…

*She takes an extra candle out of a bag on the table, then starts to light the 17 candles – now sticking out of bits of cake on top of the box of ashes.*

LISA: Come on all start singing… 'happy shit birthday to you'…

*SCOTT jumps up and runs out with the box; the bits of cake and candles, some still lit, on top of it.*

LISA: Scott!

DANIEL: Leave him – you've gone too far. I shouldn't have told you.

LISA: Scott – Scott! If you don't come back here now lad you'll never set foot over this door again – do you hear me?! I mean it lad. Scott!

LEO: *(Standing.)* I hate you mum! That was out of order.

*LEO exits. Pause. LISA sits down. She and DANIEL stare at each other. The sound of the car engine starting up.*

DANIEL: That's the car! He must have me frigging keys!

LISA: What?

*They jump up, running out. We can hear LISA and DANIEL shouting at the boys imploring them to stop; 'Eh – what the frig are you doing?' – 'Stop it now I said' – 'Come back here now youse'… 'Scott – stop it now'…the sound of the car crashing into the side of the driveway wall; general commotion and then the boys being dragged out of the car. They re-enter into the kitchen, all wet from the rain; DANIEL is holding LEO and LISA is pushing SCOTT, still clutching on the box of ashes.*

LEO: I was tryna stop him dad!

DANIEL: He tried to fucking kill me!

LEO: I didn't!

DANIEL: Not you – Scott – you tried to fucking kill me – you're a fucking nutter – you fucking psychopath!

LISA: Shut up!

DANIEL: Drove right in to me – he did!

LISA: No he didn't. Anyway you stood in front o' the car.

DANIEL: That's not the point! I was trying to stop them from driving off in the Mondeo – stupid! What did you want me to do?! Fucking nutter!

LISA: Well you're all right aren't you? – in one piece – he didn't run you over.

DANIEL: Only 'cause he crashed in to the bleeding wall! Otherwise – I'd be dead!

LISA: What were you tryna do Scott? Where the fuck did you think you were going? You've never steered a kite – never mind a car! What were you thinking?

LEO: He's had driving lessons! – he told me.

LISA: No he hasn't.

LEO: You have, haven't you Scott? Tell her…

SCOTT: Some.

LEO: How many?

SCOTT: About…two.

LEO: Shit.

DANIEL: He wasn't thinking anyway, Lisa – he never does. And as for you *(To LEO.)* – what the hell were you doing getting in the car with him?

LEO: I was trying to get him to stop! I thought I could make him…

DANIEL: You're the one with the private education!

LISA: Well he ought to know better then…

DANIEL: That's what I'm saying!

LISA: I don't think Scott took him hostage at gun-point!

DANIEL: I'm gonna check on the Mondeo. I bet it's a write-off now!

*He exits.*

LISA: What were you doing Scott?

LEO: He wanted to…he wanted to…he was going to his mum's house.

LISA: What for? She's not there?

*Pause.*

Don't you understand that? You're only upsetting yourself.

LEO: I think you upset him, just now.

LISA: I know I did. I'm sorry hon'.

*She puts her hand on him.*

You can't go breaking in to cars.

LEO: Especially not the Mondeo. Dad'll never get over it.

LISA: He'll have to.

LEO: He won't…you never touch his car.

*Re-enter DANIEL.*

DANIEL: The right hand side's all dented and scratched. I'll have to take it down the garage tomorrow. God knows what the neighbours must think…I'm surprised they haven't called the bizzies. Wouldn't be a bad thing if they did. You are a nutter!

LISA: Lay off him now Daniel.

DANIEL: You could have killed me – you almost did – and if our Leo – it's a good job I stopped 'em – eh, if he'd have taken off in that car with our Leo inside – I tell you now, I'd have a lost son. Good job.

LEO: You saved my life dad.

DANIEL: Don't try and be funny about this! That daft get would have killed you – I'm telling you now. Car crash deaths are not very nice.

LISA: Well – I almost lost all my sons – both o' them – but they're both still here – in one piece – nice and safe…only emotional scars, maybe…

DANIEL: Our Leo could have been killed – that's all I'm telling you.

LISA: And our Scott! There are two of them, you know.

DANIEL: *(At SCOTT.)* He's the one who went driving off like a bleeding maniac! It's our Leo I'm worried about.

LISA: It's the car you're worried about!

DANIEL: Don't give me that – he is my son, after all. Sorry for being over-protective – sorry for not wanting him to get killed!

LISA: Well – that's how I feel about both of them. Now you know!

DANIEL: It is only natural Lis' – that I should put my own son in mind first, you know – it's not a crime! What decent parent wouldn't?

LISA: Decent? *(Standing.)* What are you trying to say?

DANIEL: You heard.

LISA: Yeh I did – so, by your definition, I care about both o' them – equally…can't you understand…you're contradicting yourself.

DANIEL: I don't understand how you can…it's only natural for a father to put his own son first…that's all I'm saying.

LISA: Oh well done you – well done for 'being natural'. Well done for following your basic, animal instincts…you've really achieved something. Give this man an OBE. I tell you what, your *Guardian* reading credentials have just gone right down the pan! A lot of fucking good you'd be – looking after sick kids in Africa. *(Mocking his voice.)*… 'look at me everyone I'm Daniel…I've gotta Ford Mondeo…I put my own kids' needs first…I'm really natural…blah, blah, blah'. Fuck off!

DANIEL: *(To LEO and DANIEL.)* Right – upstairs you two – now! Go on. And don't be going anywhere!

LEO: Where would we be going?

DANIEL: Stay in that room I said! And shut the door behind you, so I know where you are!

*The boys exit, SCOTT clutching on to the box.*

I can't believe you're turning this on to me. You made him do that – all that 'call me mother' crap. You're the one who gave him up for adoption – I mean it was actually Carol who brought him up…

LISA: Oh so I'm the bad bitch all of a sudden? You were calling him all kinds a minute a go – psychopath, you called him!

DANIEL: Our Leo should o' known better than to get in that car with him. I knew puttin' them both in that room was a bad idea.

LISA: I'm not giving up me little gym.

DANIEL: I don't see why not? The only time you go in there is to hoover it! You should open it up to the public – start selling membership cards. The equipment's not been used.

LISA: They need to be together.

DANIEL: Rubbish Lis'. That Scott needs his own space – his own head space for one.

LISA: It's getting him out o' that that's the problem. I need him to come out of himself.

DANIEL: Yeh – well I think from what we've seen tonight – he's one jack that's better off back in his box.

LISA: Being with Leo is good for him.

DANIEL: Good for him maybe – not for us! Not for Leo neither.

LISA: They've spent their entire lives apart – I want them to be together.

DANIEL: By rights at their age they should be arguing all the time.

LISA: They do argue.

DANIEL: You're joking aren't you? Look at them tonight. They've formed an alliance – Bonny and Clyde – united against us…look at us now…

LISA: I told you it was a bad idea sending him to that school. He's not ready for that kind of academic pressure.

DANIEL: Blame me, for trying to help.

LISA: I am doing! He doesn't even seem to know that Carol's actually dead – I don't know where he was during her cremation – and you want him to get his head around the theory of relativity…

DANIEL: He was there – at the cremation.

LISA: Physically Daniel yes – his mind wasn't.

DANIEL: I'm not surprised…must be…what are we gonna do?

*They sit, thinking.*

LISA: Can you smell something…

DANIEL: What – mouse shit?

LISA: No – I think I can smell…burning.

*DANIEL jumps up and goes out to the hallway.*

Get out here now Lisa!

LISA: Hold on!

*She runs out.*

DANIEL: There's something – phone the fire service – get some tea-towels – oh Jesus!

*Fade.*

## SCENE 2

*The next morning; Saturday. LISA is scrubbing and cleaning in the kitchen. Enter DANIEL, carrying a sports bag; initially she does not see him. He hides the sports-bag down by his side.*

LISA: Oh it's you. I've bleached this place twice over now – the fridge is as good as new. Should be all right now. I'll pop down and get me new shopping in later – some bits. Still no sign o' that mouse.

DANIEL: It'll be gone by now.

LISA: I don't know. *(Looking around the floor.)* What happened, anyway?

DANIEL: What?

LISA: The car?

DANIEL: Oh. They'll give me a quote later. Gonna be expensive.

LISA: Are we insured?

*Pause. LISA starts sorting the washing out.*

DANIEL: Has he said anything?

LISA: Not much. He's been very quiet. The silence of the lambs.

DANIEL: Did you get any sleep?

LISA: No. Well, a bit – you know…on the sofa. I wasn't leaving him. He was quite happy kippin' on the fold-up, in there;

not that he had much choice. Anyway our Leo was made up o' course – sleeping in his tent.

DANIEL: Doesn't really count.

LISA: Yeh well – I wasn't letting him go outside.

DANIEL: That is the point of a tent.

LISA: Too cold; anyway I think we've had enough risk for one life-time, don't you? *(Looking out of the window.)* We've certainly given the conservatory committee plenty to talk about. *(Rummaging through dirty washing.)* Anyway, look, I told our Leo to get back handy, look – I thought it might be nice, you know, well, I thought we might have a little family outing today, you know – just around town. I haven't been to the new museum yet – our Leo'll love that. What do you think? I just thought it be nice for us, you know…

*Pause.*

You haven't got anything planned have you? You like all that sight-seeing stuff.

DANIEL: I know – I just…I'm not ready.

LISA: Daniel come on – it's just, what we need.

*Pause.*

LISA: What's the bag for?

DANIEL: I just…I'm gonna stay at me ma's…

*Pause.*

I'll get the bus up. Give me a chance, well, you know – it'll give me a chance to, to get me head straight. Our Leo's coming, he said…be nice for him to spend a couple o' nights at his nan's…

LISA: Well thanks for fucking discussing it!

DANIEL: I am discussing it – now.

*Silence.*

LISA: So that's it…we've got a situation…and this is what…
like, you're just gonna run off…and leave me in the shit.
Thanks Daniel; don't worry about me – I'll deal with it on
me own, thanks…

DANIEL: I just thought…I thought…God, look, it's just for a
couple o' nights – give you and Scott some space…some
time to…

LISA: Space? Space for him to do what, exactly – start an even
bigger fire?

DANIEL: Yeh…well…I don't wanna be here when he does.

LISA: Oh great.

DANIEL: Look…I know it was an accident Lis'.

LISA: What – Scott's conception? Not exactly.

DANIEL: You know what I mean!

LISA: Settin' fire to the duvet was an accident. Not the other…

DANIEL: Yeh – I know.

*Pause.*

Oh hell; I don't know wha' I'm doing!

*He puts down the bag and paces up and down the kitchen.*

What's happening here?

LISA: You might come back to a pile o' cinders…

DANIEL: Christ. A bit weird, isn't? Setting fire to his mother's
ashes. The poor woman's already been cremated. What
more does he want?

LISA: He wanted to…he couldn't get the lid off; he said. It's
sealed – screwed down. He wanted to, you know…I don't
know…he was curious; or something. He wanted to…
see…what was inside. He tried to get it open – by burning
the lid off.

DANIEL: He knows what was inside.

74

LISA: No, I mean – you know…he wanted…he wanted to, see what the' looked like. That's what he said.

DANIEL: Morbid get.

LISA: He's only a kid Daniel. It's just his way…

*Pause.*

DANIEL: Anyway, it's just a couple o' nights.

LISA: It'll only take him a couple o' seconds to light another match! Talk about a health and safety hazard. I need International Rescue on the scene – and you're pissing off to Maghull! The only thing that's gonna be left of any of us is that bleeding snake – crawling out, from under the ashes…

DANIEL: You paint a vivid picture Lisa. Look – I'm not sticking round here, right, unless he gets some counseling. It's a simple as that. By the sounds of it, he bloody well needs it all right…

LISA: Counseling? You won't be happy until this entire family's put in a collective straight-jacket!

DANIEL: Yeh well – better than a collective urn.

LISA: What about the ashes?

DANIEL: What about them?

LISA: We need to scatter them…like the woman asked for.

DANIEL: Good luck with that.

LISA: What about her family?

DANIEL: What about Scott?

LISA: We need to tell them…he won't part with them.

DANIEL: That's exactly why counseling…

LISA: All right Sigmund Freud!

DANIEL: I mean, what's he gonna do next – stab us all in our beds?

LISA: Don't be stupid.

DANIEL: You don't know though do you? You've never dealt with a kid like this before.

LISA: Exactly. Don't go jumping to conclusions.

DANIEL: I mean he's already started setting fire to things. Better to be safe than sorry.

*Pause.*

*(Looking at his watch.)* Look, I'll see you later, anyway.

*He looks at LISA, then leaves. She stands, staring out of the window. Silence. She turns on the radio and gets annoyed trying to find the station she wants. She almost goes to smash the radio, but stops herself. Pause. Enter SCOTT. She turns the radio off.*

SCOTT: All right?

*Pause.*

Where's Leo?

LISA: At Mally's.

*Pause.*

SCOTT: Are we going in to town then?

LISA: No Scott. We're not going in to town.

SCOTT: Oh. I'll get back on with me English then.

LISA: You won't be getting you're new bedding today, either.

SCOTT: Oh. Why?

LISA: Because we haven't got the car. You'll have to go back to Thomas the Tank Engine.

*Pause.*

SCOTT: Can I help…do you want me to do anything?

*Pause.*

LISA: Dry these dishes.

*They work together without talking. Fade.*

*Later that day in the boys' room. There may be some superficial damage around from where Scott set fire to his duvet, which has since been replaced with the Thomas the Tank Engine one from earlier. SCOTT sits on his bed with Dave's tank next to him. He is watching the old film of the 'The Importance of Being Earnest' on his laptop. We hear the line… 'To lose one parent may be regarded as a misfortune, to lose both looks like carelessness'. On the floor is the box of ashes – a little charred and damaged, but still unopened. Enter LEO. SCOTT closes his laptop.*

SCOTT: All right. Where've you been?

LEO: Out.

*LEO starts to pack a bag.*

SCOTT: What are you doing?

*Pause.*

I tidied up. Thought it was getting a bit…anyway – hope it's better.

LEO: I wish you wouldn't.

SCOTT: Wish I wouldn't what?

LEO: Tidy; move me things…you've got your own desk now, haven't you? You don't need to…just leave my stuff alone, will you? I don't like people touching my things.

SCOTT: Sorry.

LEO: Where have you put my Physics book?

SCOTT: Over there.

*Pause as LEO gets his book then continues to pack.*

LEO: Is that all you ever do – play with that snake?

SCOTT: Dave, you mean.

LEO: And do we have to have that sitting there? *(Pointing to Carol's ashes.)* – gives me the creeps like…proper badly. Can't you at least…hide it…you're good at that.

*Pause.*

SCOTT: Why are you packing?

*Pause.*

I asked your mum if…I said, you need this place to yourself…I asked if she'd move me, you know, into the spare room.

LEO: Like I care. It's a bit late now, anyway.

SCOTT: What do you mean?

LEO: You've already damaged everything.

SCOTT: It's okay, isn't it? Anyway I think she's gonna move us…I mean me.

LEO: Hope so.

*Pause.*

SCOTT: Is it because o' me – you're going?

LEO: I'm going to me nan's, that's all. Me dad's there.

SCOTT: How you getting there?

LEO: He's picking me up – any minute.

SCOTT: How long you goin' for?

LEO: I don't know.

*Pause.*

SCOTT: Oh don't go…come on…do you wanna go campin' tomorrow? You could show me…

LEO: Oh yeh – where we gonna do that then – Asda carpark?

SCOTT: I thought…you know where we could go…

LEO: It's not the time of…it's a bad idea Scott. Like everything. Anyway if I was gonna go camping I'd go with somebody…I wouldn't go with you. You need to know what you're doing.

SCOTT: You could teach me.

LEO: Whatever.

SCOTT: Was it good, in your tent last night?

LEO: Okay – I didn't…I was just testing it…okay…I wouldn't sleep in a tent – in-doors. I'm not like…5 years old.

*SCOTT gets out his phone and plays the tune from 'Thomas the Tank Engine' to amuse LEO, but it doesn't.*

SCOTT: I thought, if I play it loud enough, your mum might get the hint…you know – get me a new cover.

LEO: Yeh well – she already did that; and you set fire to it.

*SCOTT just lies on his bed watching LEO as he finishes his packing.*

SCOTT: See you in school then?

LEO: Yeh – except…please…look, don't come over to me, if I'm with my mates…okay…and yeh – it is because…and don't put *your* drinks down on *my* desk…use your own.

*LEO goes to exit and SCOTT jumps up and goes over to him.*

SCOTT: Please – don't go to your nan's. Stay. Let's go to the pictures, or something…we'll have a laugh…

LEO: Let me go Scott!

SCOTT: Come on bro'. *(Putting his arm on LEO.)*

LEO: Don't do that!

*LEO pushes SCOTT away, violently. SCOTT falls to the floor.*

I'm not your brother – right! You make me feel like, proper sick; touching that snake all the time – don't ever touch me!

*Slight pause.*

I shouldn't be alone with you. I don't even know why I'm talking to you. Just…piss off will you?!

*Slight pause.*

Me dad's right – you're a fucking nut case; there's
something wrong with you lad – you're not right in the
head!

*Slight pause.*

Everything was fine…we were happy…till you turned up…
you and that fucking snake. Now – it's like a nut-house in
here – then you nearly burn me room down!

SCOTT: I didn't mean to Leo. It was an accident.

*Pause.*

I'm sorry. Please.

LEO: I'm sorry as well. Sorry you exist.

*Slight pause.*

Look, I don't want you still in me room when I get back
– if you haven't burnt it down. And get that fucking snake
out as well – and that thing! *(Pointing to the ashes.)*

*LEO exits. Silence. SCOTT's phone plays the 'Thomas the Tank
Engine' theme-tune again. Fade.*


## SCENE 4

*A week later. A re-union dinner. LISA and DANIEL setting up a meal
in the kitchen, as at the start, quickly moving about.*

LISA: We better call them soon.

DANIEL: 'Come on down'!

LISA: Have you told Leo, about tonight?

DANIEL: What? – I think he knows we're having dinner; I
mean, we usually do.

LISA: *You* know what I mean.

DANIEL: No I don't.

LISA: You do.

DANIEL: Okay then.

LISA: So have you told him? We agreed.

DANIEL: I don't know – 'cause I don't know what you're going on about.

LISA: Daniel – oh for God's – the whole purpose of – you know – what we're gonna do, tonight – you know – what we're gonna say…to Scott.

DANIEL: Oh yeh.

*Pause.*

No; I haven't told him.

LISA: Why not – we agreed?!

DANIEL: Did we?

LISA: Yes! Remember – we approach this as a family.

DANIEL: We're not the frigging Brady Bunch. I'm sorry –I didn't tell him.

LISA: Why not?

DANIEL: Because I forgot?! Too busy worrying about – everything else.

LISA: Right. This is ready. You pour this out – I'll get them down.

*DANIEL puts out the dinner – mushroom risotto again, and LISA calls the boys.*

Come on down lads!

DANIEL: 'Come on down'!

LISA: Come on it's ready!

DANIEL: 'It's ready'…

*Silence as DANIEL puts the dinner out and LEO enters, followed by SCOTT, carrying DAVE in his tank. The boys are not talking to each other, and both appear to be sulking. They sit down, SCOTT placing DAVE's tank in the corner. Pause.*

LISA: Erm…it's just dinner for four tonight, Scott.

SCOTT: What?

LISA: I think you should leave Dave upstairs.

*Pause.*

SCOTT: Oh. Okay.

*SCOTT gets up and takes DAVE's tank upstairs, which pleases LEO. Silence; DANIEL and LISA still laying things out and putting food on the plates. SCOTT returns and sits down. Everything is ready and now everyone is sitting in place.*

DANIEL: Do you want me to say grace tonight?

LISA: Who are we now then – The Waltons?

DANIEL: Yes.

LISA: Well Scott – your favourite.

SCOTT: Oh yeh. 'Mushroom risotto'.

LISA: And…

*She gets up and takes a saucer from off the top of a bowl, revealing a plate of chips.*

Just for you.

SCOTT: Are these for me?

LISA: Just for you.

DANIEL: Can I have some?

SCOTT: Yeh.

LISA: No – these are just for our Scott.

*Slight pause.*

Eat up then!

LEO: That's not fair. Why does he get chips, and not me?

LISA: You didn't ask for none.

LEO: Neither did he. I didn't know you was making chips, anyway.

82

SCOTT: You can have some o' mine.

LEO: No thanks.

SCOTT: Go on…have some.

*SCOTT puts some chips on to LEO's plate. They eat in silence.*

DANIEL: Well, good news about the spare room, eh? You pleased to be getting your own room then eh, Scott?

SCOTT: Defo.

LEO: I certainly am.

LISA: No-one asked you.

DANIEL: Yis never did like them bunk beds…

LISA: Shut it you…they did…they do like them.

LEO: No we don't mum.

LISA: No-one asked you.

*Silence as they eat.*

LEO: What's me mum gonna do with all her exercise equipment?

DANIEL: *(Slight pause as he chews.)* Sell it on eBay.

*She gives him a sharp a look.*

You've never used any of it. Must be worth a few bob.

*Pause.*

It'll have to go in the shed.

LISA: No way. It'll get rusty in there.

DANIEL: Where else…

LISA: In our room…

DANIEL: Oh great. It can't all go in there.

LISA: Some of it…the bike can.

DANIEL: You know I'm gonna trip over that thing in the night, don't ya?

LISA: I don't care.

DANIEL: You will when I wake you up, screaming me head off.

LISA: You'll just have to get used it.

LEO: Like when someone takes over your room, with a snake.

LISA: Shut it you…don't start!

LEO: Start what?

LISA: See – I told you; you should o'told him!

LEO: Told me what?

*Pause.*

Anyway, I'm the one living with 'voodoo child'.

LISA: Stop moaning. He's moving out, isn't he?

LEO: About time…

LISA: Shut up about it now.

*They continue eating in silence.*

DANIEL: Leo, why don't you go upstairs, for a bit…

LEO: Me – why?

LISA: No!

*Slight pause.*

I want him to stay here.

*Slight pause.*

I said…we're a family, aren't we…

LEO: I don't like the sound o' this.

LISA: Sound o' what?

LEO: All this 'family' business. It's weird. I think I will go upstairs. *(He gets up.)*

LISA: Sit down you!

LEO: What?

DANIEL: Lisa – he's not prepared…I should have…

LEO: Prepared for what?

LISA: Sit down Leo – now!

*Pause. He sits down. Silence.*

LISA: Scott – now listen…now, I know it's been hard for you. Very…you've had it tough lad…but, you're here, with us now.

*Pause.*

We need to…we're gonna…scatter your mum's ashes… tonight…as a family…it's what she asked for. Look, we'll drive down the river…

*SCOTT jumps up and exits to his room. LISA stands up and calls him.*

LISA: Scott! Scott!

*Pause.*

I should go up.

DANIEL: No. Just leave him.

*Pause.*

Give him a break, eh.

*Pause.*

*LISA sits down. LEO jumps up.*

DANIEL: Where are you going?

*He does not answer and exits to his room. LISA calls after him.*

LISA: Leo! Leo!

*Cut to SCOTT in his room, pacing up and down. LEO enters and just watches him; SCOTT pays no attention, kicking DAVE's tank; 'I hope you fucking die!' He picks up the box of ashes. In anger and frustration he attempts to wrench it open with his fingers, but gets nowhere, becoming increasingly desperate, tearful, and pathetic.*

*He collapses on to the floor. Pause. LEO goes to the desk, picks up a screw-driver then hands it to SCOTT. SCOTT looks at it for a while, then uses it to open the box; eventually the lid comes off. He stands up and scatters the ashes out of the skylight, in to the night sky.*

*Fade.*